AF304896

Praise for *Building Great Businesses*

"Scott Becker has long been a trusted counsel of the healthcare and business ecosystem—the rare voice who both understands and amplifies the operators shaping the industry's future. His new book, *Building Great Businesses*, distills decades of hard-earned insight and relationships into a playbook for navigating business building in complex industries."

> —Julie Yoo, general partner with
> Andreessen Horowitz

"As someone who has spent a career partnering with growth-minded companies, I can say *Building Great Businesses* captures the principles that truly separate top performers from everyone else. Scott's experience across healthcare, business, and leadership makes this an essential guide for builders at every stage of business."

> —Justin Ishbia, founder of Shore Capital and
> partner and part majority owner of the
> Phoenix Suns and Phoenix Mercury

"*Building Great Businesses* is classic Scott Becker—smart, direct, and grounded in real experience. Scott has a deep understanding of what it takes to build momentum, overcome challenges, and lead through complexity. This book is a must-read for founders, operators, and investors who want to build with purpose and confidence."

> —Anthony Scaramucci, founder and managing
> partner of SkyBridge Capital, founder and
> chairman of the SALT Conference

"Scott Becker brings the same clarity, insight, and strategic depth to *Building Great Businesses* that he has brought to his clients and colleagues for decades. This book is a thoughtful guide to leadership, growth, and navigating complexity—grounded in real experience and written with Scott's trademark generosity and wisdom. A fantastic resource for anyone building or leading an organization."

—Amber Walsh, partner and executive committee member with McGuireWoods LLP

"Scott Becker brings uncommon clarity, discipline, and real-world insight to *Building Great Businesses*. I've had the privilege of advising Scott over the years, and this book reflects the same thoughtful, principled approach he brings to building and leading. It's a practical and inspiring guide for anyone committed to building something outstanding."

—Andy Friedman, founder and former CEO, SkinnyPop, advisor, investor, and board member

"I've had the privilege of serving on a board with Scott Becker and have seen firsthand his clarity, discipline, and commitment to helping leaders succeed. *Building Great Businesses* captures the practical wisdom Scott brings to every discussion. It's a valuable guide for anyone focused on building strong, resilient organizations."

—Andrew Hayek, co-founder and CEO of Triple Aim Partners

"Scott Becker has an extraordinary ability to make complex ideas clear and actionable. *Building Great Businesses* is filled with practical insights, grounded wisdom, and the kind of strategic thinking leaders need today. Scott understands how culture, communication, and disciplined execution come together to build organizations that last."

—Marion Crawford, CEO and founder of Crawford

"Scott Becker has a genuinely unique ability to translate experience into practical wisdom. *Building Great Businesses* is a concise, powerful guide for anyone building or scaling a company. It's the kind of book that founders and investors could leverage on a daily basis."

—Venkat Mocherla, founder of Midstream
Health, investor, former Andreessen Horowitz

"Having served on boards with Scott—and having had him serve on one of mine years ago—I've seen firsthand how he thinks about leadership, teamwork, and building strong organizations. *Building Great Businesses* captures that mindset beautifully. It's practical, thoughtful, and rooted in real experience. A terrific resource for leaders at any stage."

—Barry Tanner, CEO of PE GI Solutions,
current CEO of Respite Home Care,
board member several companies

"Scott and I have known each other since our college and Harvard Law School years, and I've had the privilege of watching his journey as a leader, builder, and advisor. *Building Great Businesses* distills the lessons he has lived—clarity, consistency, and the ability to make smart decisions under pressure. It's a valuable guide for anyone working to lead well."

—Nancy Temple, managing
partner of Katten Temple

"If 'business as usual' is your plan, skip this book. If you're ready to build what's next and stay human while you do it, start here. I've seen Scott turn complexity into choices you can act on by Monday. This book packages that clarity for every builder."

—Stephen K. Klasko, MD, MBA, executive
in residence with General Catalyst and
former CEO of Jefferson Health

"Scott Becker brings clarity, purpose, and practical wisdom in *Building Great Businesses*. Having worked with Scott in several capacities, including his service on the board of National Medical Fellowships, I've seen firsthand his deep commitment to leadership that is grounded in integrity and impact. This book offers a thoughtful and accessible road map for anyone striving to build organizations that excel."

—Michellene Davis, CEO of National
Medical Fellowships

"Scott Becker has spent decades helping leaders think bigger, execute smarter, and build businesses that endure. *Building Great Businesses* distills his wisdom into practical, actionable insights that speak directly to entrepreneurs, healthcare leaders, and anyone navigating growth and change. Scott's voice is grounded, generous, and deeply experienced—this book will leave readers more confident, more intentional, and better equipped to build something meaningful."

—Nisha Mehta, MD, founder of Physician Side Gigs

"Every once in a while, there is a generational talent that comes along that allows us to fully comprehend the intricacies and details that are necessary to build and run a great business. Scott Becker, founder of Becker's Healthcare, is one of those individuals. His uncanny business acumen and expertise has allowed him to build and run a true healthcare business empire. His new book, *Building Great Businesses*, is filled with practical wisdom and clear lessons that resonate far beyond business. Scott Becker delivers real insight into leadership, discipline, and building organizations that last. A valuable read for anyone striving to lead and improve."

—Michael R. Redler, MD, orthopedic
surgeon and healthcare leader

"As an entrepreneur, author, speaker, and former CIO, I appreciate books that translate experience into action. In *Building Great Businesses*, Scott Becker offers exactly that—clear principles, smart strategies, and timeless lessons for leaders who want to grow with purpose. I plan to gift copies to all my peer board members. This is the kind of book you keep within arm's reach."

—Edward Marx, founder and CEO of Marx Advisory

"Scott Becker's *Building Great Businesses* is a smart, practical guide for anyone leading, building, or reinventing an organization. His insights are clear, actionable, and grounded in real experience. A terrific read for entrepreneurs and leaders across healthcare and beyond."

—Scott Sigman, MD, orthopedic surgeon
and healthcare entrepreneur

"Scott Becker has an extraordinary ability to simplify complexity and illuminate what truly drives great companies. *Building Great Businesses* reflects the same wisdom, integrity, and long-term thinking I've seen in Scott throughout the many years we've worked together. This book is a must-read for leaders who want to build with purpose, resilience, and clarity."

—Nader Samii, chairman of the
board of Nimble Solutions

"Scott Becker brings exceptional clarity and hard-earned wisdom to *Building Great Businesses*. Having served with Scott on the board of Regent Surgical Health, I've seen firsthand his deep understanding of leadership, strategy, and what it truly takes to build durable organizations. This book captures those insights and delivers them in a practical, accessible way. A valuable read for entrepreneurs, executives, and investors alike."

—Tom Mallon, cofounder of Regent Surgical
Health and founder of Perpetuate Capital

"Scott Becker is one of the rare leaders whose wisdom is both practical and deeply grounded in experience. In *Building Great Businesses*, he delivers the clear, steady guidance that has made him a trusted voice to so many of us over the years. As someone who appreciates a bit of British understatement, I'll simply say this: Scott gets it right. This book is thoughtful, timely, and genuinely useful for any founder or leader."

—Holly Buckley, chair of Healthcare
Department at McGuireWoods LLP

"*Building Great Businesses* is a masterclass on what it takes to build with purpose and establish a lasting institution. Scott constantly surrounds himself with the best leaders and has distilled a very unique set of experiences into clear, practical insights for anyone interested in building a generational business. In the endless sea of business books, this stands out—I commend Scott on sharing his unique learnings."

—Manav Sevak, founder and CEO
of Memora Health

"Scott Becker understands business, leadership, and resilience at a depth very few do. *Building Great Businesses* captures the real work of building something meaningful—navigating risk, aligning people, and staying disciplined through cycles. This book is wise, energizing, and grounded in lessons that actually matter. I'm proud to recommend it."

—Dutch Rojas, investor, builder, healthcare
innovator, and strategic thinker

"Scott Becker's *Building Great Businesses* is a practical and insightful guide for leaders navigating growth, complexity, and constant change. His lessons are grounded in real experience and delivered with rare clarity. This book is an excellent resource for entrepreneurs and executives who want to build durable, high-performing organizations."

—Sherri Douville, CEO of Medigram

"As an auctioneer and business leader, I've seen what strong judgment and steady leadership look like. Scott Becker brings both to *Building Great Businesses*. Having known Scott for decades, I can say this book is a true reflection of who he is—thoughtful, hardworking, and focused on helping others build well."

—Rick Levin, founder and CEO of
Rick Levin and Associates

"I've had the privilege of learning, leading, and building alongside Scott Becker for decades. *Building Great Businesses* reflects the same qualities he brings to every client and partnership—incisive clarity, uncompromising integrity, and a deep wisdom that drives real, sustained success. Scott's impact on my career and life is a tribute to these virtues put into practice. This book is filled with practical insights and lessons earned through experience which can be applied broadly. It's an invaluable guide for leaders at any stage. I will be giving a copy to each of my future leaders."

—Bart Walker, partner, with McGuireWoods LLP

"Serving alongside Scott Becker has given me a front-row seat to his clarity, consistency, and deep understanding of what makes organizations thrive. *Building Great Businesses* is filled with practical insights leaders can use immediately. It reflects the thoughtful, steady guidance Scott brings to every boardroom."

—Kelley Blair, CEO of Nimble Solutions

"I've had the privilege of working closely with Scott Becker for many years and have been able to gain excellent insights from observing him build and run his businesses. I have also received a lot of invaluable advice from him on running and growing the company I founded. *Building Great Businesses* captures the clarity, discipline, and genuine leadership he brings to every project. This practical book is filled with many of the same strategies and lessons he has taught me over the years that helped me make my business what it is today. This book is an excellent guide for anyone looking to build something great. If you follow the advice offered here, it will work for you like it worked for me."

—Jeremy Corr, founder and CEO of
Executive Podcast Solutions

"Scott Becker has a rare ability to distill complex ideas into practical, usable wisdom and has long been willing to share his insights. *Building Great Businesses* captures his clarity, discipline, and genuine commitment to helping others succeed spurred along by his terrific guidance. I've had the pleasure of working alongside Scott for many years, and his insights here mirror the thoughtful, steady leadership he consistently demonstrates. This book is a powerful guide for anyone trying to build, grow, or rebuild a business, something that Scott has repeatedly done so incredibly well—and it reflects Scott at his absolute best. A true credit to Scott for continuing to be willing to share his helpful perspectives with others in the hopes of building their success."

—David Pivnick, partner with McGuireWoods LLP

"I've known Scott for almost forty years. Without question, he's one of the brightest and hardest-working people

I know. More importantly, he's rare in how practical and direct he is. No fluff; he thinks in a straight line and gets right to the point. This book is a succinct collection of his 'lessons learned' over the last forty years in not only advising companies in corporate/strategic transactions, but in building up Becker's Healthcare from scratch to what it is today. This book is immediately useful for anyone building or leading an organization."

    —William Crawford, CEO of Pacolet
    Milliken Enterprises

"*Building Great Businesses* is a master class in leadership, resilience, and momentum. Scott Becker distills decades of experience into lessons that are practical, timeless, and deeply usable. His clarity of thought and commitment to helping others grow come through on every page. His concepts are insightful, actionable, and based on real-world experience. This book is essential reading for anyone building or scaling an organization."

    —Michelle Byers-Robson, co-owner of SCORAH

"Scott Becker has dedicated his career to empowering leaders to think critically and build with intention. In *Building Great Businesses*, he distills his insights into a compelling narrative that is both practical and inspiring. This book serves as an invaluable resource for anyone striving to lead effectively and scale their ventures with confidence. Scott's wisdom not only illuminates the path to successful leadership but also instills a sense of purpose that is essential in today's dynamic business environment."

    —Will Conaway, healthcare strategist

"Scott Becker has been a trusted colleague and friend whose perspective I greatly appreciate His new book, *Building Great Businesses*, is a reflection of the practical wisdom, encouragement, and grounded guidance he's offered for years. Scott's insights help leaders stay focused on what truly matters, and I'm proud to endorse this work."
—Dr. Imamu Tomlinson,MD, MBA, CEO of
Vituity, and author of *Less Than One Percent*

"When I think of Scott Becker, three things come to mind: integrity, generosity, and a tireless drive to help others succeed. *Building Great Businesses* is Scott in a nutshell—practical, insightful, and rooted in real experience. He's had a genuine impact on my career, and I'm thrilled to recommend this book."
—Lisa Rock, founder of National Medical Billing

"After thirty years working with Scott Becker, I continue to be impressed with his grasp of the changing landscape of business. His insight is invaluable and spans industries, from his work in the rapidly changing healthcare industry to his interaction with world leaders and business leaders through his media company. Scott continues to be a steady, trusted voice in business. In *Building Great Businesses*, he shares practical, real-world wisdom that leaders can immediately apply. Scott's clarity, discipline, and deep understanding of how organizations grow make this book an invaluable guide for anyone striving to build something great."
—Joe Zasa, managing principal
for ASD Management

"Scott is the best out there, and having his insights—earned through direct, lived experiences building businesses—on building momentum, scaling, and overcoming setbacks (there will be many) synthesized into a book is priceless. No matter where you are in your business-building journey, the principles covered here, if applied, will alter your trajectory for the better."

—Travis Guerra, founder and CEO of ONWARD

BUILDING GREAT BUSINESSES

BUILDING GREAT BUSINESSES

CREATE MOMENTUM, OVERCOME SETBACKS, AND SCALE WITH CONFIDENCE

SCOTT BECKER

WITH MOLLY GAMBLE

Forefront
BOOKS

CONTENTS

CONTENTS

FOREWORD
by Jessica Cole

There's a popular exercise I learned from the Young Presidents' Organization—commonly referred to as YPO—called your 5/5/5: Who are the five most influential people in your life? What are the five most influential events? What are the five biggest accomplishments? Somehow, Scott Becker is woven into all three of those for me.

Working alongside Scott for nearly two decades has shaped me as a leader, a professional, and a person in ways that are impossible to fully express. Our journey together has been intense, fun, challenging, and deeply meaningful—full of lessons that continue to guide how I think, work, and lead.

I'll admit, I skip the foreword in most books. But if you read no further, know this: This book is absolutely worth your time. My measure of a great book is whether you walk away with two or three solid takeaways. You'll finish this one with far more than that.

From an early age, I had an unusual drive to work. I truly loved it. My family jokingly nicknamed me "Little Miss Workerpants" when I was around five years old—a name that stuck far longer than they probably expected. I always wanted to help, to be useful, to take initiative, and to tackle challenges. That instinct—to show up and give my best—became the foundation of everything that followed.

My first real job was at Hy-Vee Drugstore, a Midwestern grocery store with the tagline "A helpful smile in every aisle." I took that to heart. Hy-Vee taught me that business, at its core, is about people—about serving others, caring about their experience, and leaving them better than when you found them. That simple lesson in customer service became one of the cornerstones of how I lead and how Becker's Healthcare operates today.

Our COO, Katie Atwood, says it best when coaching our teammates before a live event: "Pretend you're in a small town. Smile at everyone. Be approachable. And constantly look for ways to help."

Later, during college, I had a transformational internship after my freshman year. I left Iowa and went on quite the adventure selling encyclopedias door-to-door in Marin County, California. There is no better classroom for grit and resilience than standing on a stranger's doorstep asking for their time and money (and occasionally a sandwich and a glass of water)—and hearing "no" a hundred times before hearing "yes."

That experience taught me how to dig deep, find intrinsic motivation, and stay positive when things were hard. It showed me that persistence is a choice you make every single day. Rent is due every day—it doesn't matter if you made five sales yesterday. You're only as good as the effort you bring today. That "good is never good enough" and mental-toughness mindset was instilled in me through that Southwestern Publishing internship, and it became a core part of how I approach work and leadership.

Throughout college, I worked in sponsorship sales, high-end jewelry, Geek Squad installs, event planning, and experience building—anything that allowed me to lead people, grow things, and accomplish goals. Whether it was organizing student fundraisers, coordinating 5Ks, or leading campus nonprofits, I loved bringing big ideas to life and motivating others to rally behind them. Without realizing it, I was building the exact tool kit I would need for the next chapter of my life at Becker's Healthcare.

I still remember the day Scott and I first spoke. He interviewed me from a noisy airport. I was working at a jewelry store. I ran back to my college apartment during a quick fifteen-minute break to take the call. We spoke for maybe seven minutes—but I was energized. I was still at the University of Iowa, interviewing with companies like Medtronic and Stryker, but I couldn't stop thinking about the opportunity Scott described.

My parents were puzzled when I told them I was turning down a medical device career to join a lawyer with a tiny team, an outsourced events company, and a big vision. They asked, more than once, "What is this? Who is this? Why do you think this is a good idea?"

But something about it felt right. The idea of joining a vision and building something from the ground up lit me up. It felt like a hunt—a challenge to prove to myself that we could do something hard and make it great. I had complete clarity: I was all in for ASC Communications, which was what we were called at the time.

Scott is, in every sense, a builder. He has an endless supply of energy and ideas—truly an idea-a-minute kind of person. In those early days, I had to try to keep up. He'd brainstorm ten new concepts in a few hours, and by the end of the day, we were running at one or two of them. But what made Scott exceptional wasn't just his creativity—it was his ability to commit and lock in. Once he chose a direction, there was no half measure. He pursued it with relentless focus until it worked—and then kept going.

Scott also had a gift for recognizing potential before it was fully visible—and, more importantly, for trusting it. That same "commit and lock in" mindset showed up in how he mentored and developed leaders. His confidence in me early on was like fuel. It felt as if someone with an extra-large gas tank was pouring energy into a small campfire every day—sparking growth and feeding it until it caught fire.

That blend of curiosity and discipline became the DNA of Becker's Healthcare. I learned that great businesses aren't built on ideas alone—they're built on the rare ability to focus, commit, and follow through.

Among the early books Scott recommended I read were three by Dr. Jason Selk: *Relentless Solution Focus*, *Organize Tomorrow Today*, and *Executive Toughness*. I've reread them countless times, and we've had Dr. Selk speak at several of our company trainings. That discipline—to attack the most important things every day—was something Scott modeled from the start. He can get more done by seven a.m. than most people do all day.

Scott also taught me what it means to always be learning. He was constantly reading—business books, biographies, history, management theory, you name it. His appetite for knowledge is unmatched. I'd often wake up to late-night emails with book recommendations or quotes he wanted to share. I realized quickly that if I wanted to keep up, I had to read as much as he did. Scott is maybe the fastest reader, thinker, and synthesizer of ideas on Earth.

When I joined Becker's, Scott was running both a law firm and the small but growing media business. He was just beginning to hire a few full-time employees and shift from an outsourced model to building a real internal team. Those were the chaotic early days of entrepreneurship—no playbook, no polish, just grit, creativity, and an unwavering belief that we could build something meaningful.

In my mid-twenties, Scott made the bold decision to put me in charge of the company. I was young, untested, and suddenly leading a team of people older and more experienced than me. We weren't a big team at all, and half of it quit immediately—but we rebuilt.

Scott's influence shaped me in profound ways. He modeled the power of clarity—focusing only on what truly matters and saying no to everything else. He loved the Peter Drucker quote, "The executive who wants to be effective says 'yes' only to the few activities that make a difference."[1] That discipline became a guiding principle for me as a leader. The first book he ever sent me (with a handwritten note, while I still lived in Iowa City) was *The Daily Drucker*. In a world overflowing with distractions, focus is one of the greatest competitive advantages.

Scott also taught me about connection. He has a mind like a steel trap—remembering names, stories, and details years later. But more than that, he has an innate ability to connect people—to see potential partnerships before anyone else can. That's been one of Becker Healthcare's greatest strengths: not just publishing ideas, but bringing people together to share, learn, and grow.

Of course, the process of building something lasting is rarely easy. There were seasons that tested us—times that required both grit and grace. But through those moments, I learned that tension often precedes transformation. Building a company and growing as a leader requires courage, patience, and the willingness to keep showing up, even when it's hard.

Over time, Scott and I developed an almost instinctive rhythm. We could finish each other's sentences, anticipate each other's thoughts, and navigate the fun and chaos of growth together. We didn't always agree, but we were always aligned on the mission: to create something meaningful, to add value, and to do great work that matters.

Scott used to say, "You have to dig ten ditches before they start to dig themselves." There are no shortcuts to momentum. You earn it—through consistency, persistence, and a commitment to the long game. That's how Becker's Healthcare was built: brick by brick, idea by idea, day by day, teammate by teammate.

Scott Becker is one of the most relentlessly curious and driven people I've ever known. He's a builder, a thinker, and a connector. He has the energy of a creator and the discipline of an operator. He taught me that leadership is equal parts learning, deciding, and staying the course—and that nothing happens without a great team.

This book captures the hard-won lessons of a life spent building, learning, and leading. It's more than a guide to business growth—it's a reflection of the mindset and principles that have guided Scott not just in building a company but in helping countless leaders and entrepreneurs navigate the challenges of growth. I'm profoundly grateful for what I've learned from him, for the opportunities he created, and for the partnership that has defined so much of my journey.

Today, we still carry the same spirit and lessons you'll read throughout this book. To our team, past and present—thank you. You are the heart of this company.

Thank you—and buckle up. You're about to dive into a collection of practical, thoughtful, and brilliant lessons that will help you grow both personally and professionally.

Jessica Cole, president and CEO,
Becker's Healthcare

INTRODUCTION

This book tells the story of building businesses over a period of thirty-plus years, and it offers advice and thoughts on how to build and scale a business today. Specifically, the book draws on my experiences building both a legal practice and a media company—but the actual businesses that I started and helped to build are not the focus here. Though those companies inform my experience, our focus will be on the advice and ideas I picked up along the way. Much of that should prove universal.

I have had some very strong successes and some real failures. I have served on the boards of highly successful companies and of firms that struggled. I have invested in startups, venture capital, and private equity funds. There again, I've had some investment wins and some that have turned to zero. You win some, you lose some.

In 1992, I started working as a lawyer at a then-mid-sized Chicago-based law firm called Ross & Hardies, which later merged into a larger law firm called

McGuireWoods. When I started at Ross & Hardies, I was nearly four years out of law school. As of this writing, thirty-plus years later, I remain a partner at McGuireWoods.

Before I joined Ross & Hardies, I practiced law at a much larger firm called Katten Muchin & Zavis. That law firm is now known as KMZ. While I learned a lot there (and worked very long hours), the most important lesson I learned was that it was much better in that time and era to originate your own clients (i.e., be a rainmaker) than to be reliant on someone else for work, even as a lawyer at a big firm.

Back in the day, if you didn't have your own clients, you were treated, as I'd often say, "like a dog." You could be a fifty-year-old partner and a fantastic lawyer, but if you didn't control or originate clients, you essentially had very little control over your time and over your professional life. Someone could essentially force you to work endlessly and take over projects at the last minute—otherwise you might be first on the layoffs list.

I never wanted to treat anyone like a dog or lay them off, but I wanted to build a client base so I wouldn't be treated like a dog myself. The growth of a practice provided some level of control over my professional life. It also provided my first early lessons in building a business.

Building a practice was fascinating and invigorating to me. I was intent on building a practice focused on a specific area, as opposed to trying to be all things to all people. I wanted the ability to focus so that I could be "on when I was on" and "off when off." For example, I didn't want to treat every social event I attended as a chance to meet clients and generate business. I felt the need to focus in a more efficient way. This led me to build a specialty niche practice. Later in the book, we will talk extensively about building niche businesses and building business-to-business businesses. My focus has always been business-to-business, or B2B.

At Ross & Hardies, I joined the healthcare department and focused on learning health law and building a healthcare practice. But my niche wasn't simply in healthcare law; that too would arguably have been too broad. Rather, my efforts focused on much more specific areas within healthcare.

I did well building a healthcare-focused legal practice. However, my real entrepreneurial success came in starting and building Becker's Healthcare over the long run. When I started on the activities that led to Becker's Healthcare, I wasn't planning on building a healthcare media business. Rather, I was trying to build a healthcare legal practice by using what would today be called "thought leadership." I wrote articles and gave speeches; I started a small website and a very rudimentary newsletter; and I started to host a small conference. This was all aimed at trying to put myself in the middle of the healthcare business and growing and branding myself as a go-to healthcare lawyer. Again, healthcare may have been the overall field, but I built the company around very specific areas—not healthcare in general.

Over time, we expanded the legal practice and the media company beyond surgery centers and into several other areas. At the legal practice, the most important expansions were into healthcare private equity, healthcare companies, and health systems. At the media company, the most important growth and expansion was into hospitals and health systems, health information technology, digital health, and revenue cycle management.

Fast-forward to today: Becker's Healthcare—the effort that started as "thought leadership"—has grown into one of the nation's leading healthcare media companies. Stay ready, and you may find success where you don't expect it!

Drawn from these experiences building a legal practice and a media business, as well as my efforts serving on boards of directors and investing in private equity and venture capital funds, this book provides relatively short chapters that interweave my advice, my thoughts, and the stories of my trials and tribulations as a business builder. I hope you find it helpful as you build your own better business.

If you have questions about any of the ideas you find here, please don't hesitate to reach out.

Getting Started

When you start building a business or practice, it can take a serious amount of effort and often years of patience before the momentum builds and it starts to feel successful. As I often say, you have to dig ten ditches before they start to dig themselves.

Jim Collins, the famous author of *Good to Great*, talks extensively in his book about building momentum and a "flywheel."

> No matter how dramatic the end result, good-to-great transformations never happen in one fell swoop. In building a great company or social sector enterprise, there is no single defining action, no grand program, no one killer innovation, no solitary lucky break, no miracle moment. Rather, the process resembles relentlessly pushing a giant, heavy

flywheel, turn upon turn, building momentum until
a point of breakthrough, and beyond.[2]

Building a startup from scratch requires tremendous
energy.

As a young lawyer building a legal practice at a mid-
sized or larger firm, you face multiple uphill battles.
Many times, older lawyers think a young lawyer should
just be handling client work and not trying to build a
practice at all. In those environments, the firm at large
and many of its lawyers would bristle at a younger lawyer
showing that kind of ambition. But if someone isn't bris-
tling at what you're doing, you may not be doing the
right thing anyway.

People may also think that client businesses aren't apt
to help young lawyers. I once asked for marketing help
from my first law firm. The person who was then running marketing explained that marketing help was only
available to more senior lawyers, or at least junior partners. When I became a junior partner, another person in
a similar role said marketing help was for senior partners
only. It became clear to me that I had to drive and own
my own marketing. Lesson learned.

Similarly, when I began building the media business,
I went to visit a healthcare finance leader who strongly
discouraged me from trying to do what I was proposing.
He essentially said there was too much competition in
the field. He thought it would be too difficult. I didn't

take that advice, but that person later became a mentor and friend.

FIVE ESSENTIALS FOR THE STARTING LINE

There are many lessons to be learned when you're getting started. Here are five essentials:

1. You need to be determined. It will take tremendous effort to really get a business going. You will need to put in a lot of effort, a lot of repetition, and a lot of thought before you start to see signs of success.

2. You need to ignore the naysayers. Or, as the all-time great Michael Jordan would say, you need to use the naysayers as fuel for your journey. There is a great adage that essentially says you aren't making an impact until you get punched in the nose. View that punch in the nose, which often comes from a competitor, as a sign that you are making progress. I also love this quote on naysayers from Lorraine Stanton: "Your vision attracts both doubters and supporters. Let their skepticism fuel your fire and refine your resolve."

3. You cannot be paralyzed by analysis. You need to get started and stick with it. Yes, you will have to make pivots—no amount of planning will prevent that. I've had many people come to me to discuss starting a business or building a practice. Many of these people never really get started. Others commit fully and get things moving. It's this latter group who tend to excel.

4. It will take some time to really build momentum and get the flywheel effect going. You will need to be determined and, at some point, acknowledge some positive signals that will help you to keep moving to the point where the business has momentum. At some point, you'll start to see things click. As I said, it takes time and a lot of work before you start to see results. There may be overnight successes, but I think they're rare. I'm certainly not one of them.

5. You need to cultivate your drive and passion. When the drive starts to build and the direction starts to take shape, you have to make the very serious, deliberate decision to pursue your business goals. In other words, you have to decide not just to have a job but to become a leader. You need to keep cultivating and doubling down on what is working and what inspires you.

Keep those points in mind as we move forward. Now that your mindset is calibrated, let's talk about your first real step: a business plan.

CHAPTER 2

The Initial Business Plan

When starting a business, the type of plan I choose depends on its purpose. For example, do you need a plan to raise outside capital? Or do you need a plan to set a direction for getting the business started? Your circumstances and immediate goals will influence the plan you make, but a plan—or a series of plans—is a necessity.

When sketching out early business plans, I love utilizing the thinking of business journalist and author Suzy Welch. Her book *10–10–10: A Life-Transforming Idea* was more aimed at life issues than business issues, but the title and thinking really resonated with me.[3] It speaks to thinking about choices and plans in terms of ten minutes, ten months, and ten years. It's about seeing where you would like the business to be. I have a hard time thinking ten years out—but I love the concept of thinking ten months out or more in an early business plan.

When you develop a business plan, you want as much clarity and simplicity as possible around:

1. What you're trying to sell or produce
2. Who your ideal customers and market are
3. Where your revenue will come from
4. What your initial costs and expenses are

I've had the most success when I've brought great clarity to the basics, and I've failed when I didn't.

THREE TYPES OF BUSINESS PLANS

I divide business plans into three core types.

1. The "starting a business" plan. In many cases, people start their business without a written plan at all. I don't recommend this. In most instances, you need some kind of core plan even to establish your own direction. It need not be very complex. But just winging it and trying to figure it out as you go can lead to a tremendous amount of wasted time and energy.

I have been in that position myself, so eager to get moving that I didn't develop enough of a core plan to start out with a firm sense of direction. Consequently, I have wasted a lot of time trying to figure it out as I go. In some cases, I spent years working on a business without a clear enough plan upfront. This is a bad idea. Even a one-page business plan can set a clear direction; it's much better than the no-business-plan approach.

By nature, I am an incrementalist. I nearly always start with a relatively simple business plan like this, then I improve and expand it over time. My core reason for writing this plan is to clarify a direction for the company, myself, and the leadership. It's not really for third parties. That very first plan for any company should be largely focused on what the company is trying to do, who it is trying to do it for, and what it will take to do it.

2. The business plan that's two to ten pages—or a little bit longer. This plan generally discusses what services or products you are going to provide and/or sell. It also speaks to how you are going to generate customers, sales, and accounts for the startup and how you plan to cover the initial and ongoing costs of operating the business. I am a huge fan of the short, two- to ten-page business plan that really focuses on the core of what you want the company to do and how. As the business grows, you may very well revise and expand this business plan as well.

I don't use a specific template for the short business plan. For all practical purposes, the most successful business efforts I have been engaged with started with a page or two of business planning that primarily focused on how to develop revenues. The next-most successful approach was in the form of a three- to ten-page memo.

3. The very extensive business plan. You may see these elaborate plans online or in the context of large consulting, venture capital, or investment firms. They often run fifty to two hundred pages.

My sense is that for most starting entrepreneurs, these are not only overkill but more of a distraction. You can spend so much time on the plan that the plan becomes the journey itself. Moreover, it can make the effort seem so expansive that it becomes very hard to actually get going. Finally, you can build such an expansive plan that it becomes very hard to complete it without a substantial amount of guesswork, estimates, and projections.

There may be times when you need a complex business plan, such as when building a business out of an existing large company or when seeking substantial venture capital funding. Or you might need it because you are doing business with new partners. In those cases, you may want to utilize the long-form business plan. However, even here, you should be able to explain the core concepts of the business in a fairly straightforward manner and in only a few pages. You must be able to describe the ideal customer and niche and explain the core means of delivering your services. You should also have a very good sense of your startup costs and of the means of reaching your target market.

PROJECTION, RISK, AND FAILURE

Jason Fried, the founder of software company 37Signals and author of *Rework*, has a wonderful quote about the projections that often go into startup business plans. His quote may be overstated . . . but when I review business plans in which there is no history or track record, I often think that he is exactly right: "Projections are just bull-shit. They're just guesses."[4]

Another great quote on long-form business plans is from Alex Osterwalder, founder and CEO of Strategyzer: "Business plans are great for execution challenges like building a new factory or expanding your sales force. However, insisting on a business plan when it comes to innovation and new ventures is a terrible idea. In fact, lengthy business plans often increase the risk of failure."[5]

My sense is that most businesses should develop a relatively short business plan that makes common sense and clearly outlines the core product or service, where revenues and sales will come from, how you will generate them, and how you will deliver the product. Then you need to get started testing and developing the business. Don't get into paralysis by analysis. As I said, this happens to would-be founders way too much.

A profound quote on getting started comes from Drew Houston, the co-founder and CEO of Dropbox: "Don't worry about failure; you only have to be right once."

At some point, founders have to abandon the planning stage and get started. They have to test and pivot and move forward. In my experience, you are far better off starting the business with a very short memorandum and core business plan and then periodically adjusting and developing your strategy and plan as you go.

SHORT PLAN SUMMARY

Here is a summary on developing a short business plan. I am a huge fan of this approach. A simple business plan should be concise, clear, and focused, covering the essential components to guide your business and communicate its vision to stakeholders.

Tips for a Simple Business Plan

- Keep it five–ten pages long, depending on complexity.
- Use clear, straightforward language—avoid jargon.
- Tailor it to your audience (e.g., investors, partners, or specific persons).
- Update it regularly as your business evolves.

I'd keep it super simple. What are you trying to build and sell? Focus your plan on building a great product and finding out how to sell and distribute it effectively.

A few great founders—such as Malinka Walaliyadde at AKASA, a healthcare AI company—have pushed me to add a "yes, but" here. I do believe in the power of a simple plan to start, but you will soon need to think in terms of how you will build infrastructure and support for engineering and sales in the long term. Ten days, ten months, ten years—if those numbers correspond to increasingly long and complex plans for your new business, you're probably on the right track.

One important final note regarding business plans: You can write the perfect business plan, but if you don't have the drive and passion to execute it, that plan is worthless.

CHAPTER 3

The Spark, the Passion, and the Motivation

SPARK

At this writing, I have developed two serious businesses and have struggled on several others. The businesses that succeeded were born from situations in which I, for all practical purposes, became so excited and obsessed that they took up a huge amount of my emotional and mental space. When I have not been fully obsessed—when I have even been so lackadaisical as to treat a business like an advanced hobby—the businesses did not thrive. In fact, they often dawdled along for years and wasted a ton of my energy and time.

Sadly, I have found it's very hard to excel without a huge drive and spark to do so. I'm not sure such a thing is measurable, but you often see it in those who are operating like a determined force of nature. For oneself, this spark and drive may come and go . . . but when it comes, you should generally follow your gut and double and triple down on it.

A quick note on hobby businesses and advanced hobbies: One great example of this is the small retail store oftentimes opened up by the spouse of a successful wife or husband. I have seen this time and time again. I can almost always predict that the business will dribble along, lose money, and ultimately fail if the person starting it is not highly driven and motivated. In essence, if the business is born more from a whim than a deep drive, it will fail.

There is a pernicious, wishful belief that a business or concept will catch fire and go viral without a tremendous effort by the founder or creator to make that happen. My sense is that this hardly ever happens without that tremendous effort. It's so rare that I often think of it as a modern myth that things just *go viral* on their own.

The first serious business effort I pursued was building my healthcare legal practice and "book of business" at the law firm. Some might call this being an "intrapreneur," or building a business within a business. My spark and drive in this effort came largely from necessity. I didn't have family money or the freedom not to work, and I wanted control over my own life. The clearest path to that control was building a legal practice. I became hyper-motivated, even obsessed with doing so.

The energy and compulsion to grow the practice came from a deep sense of need—probably even fear. It also became a great challenge and a fascinating game as I grew the practice and aimed for and developed goals for it.

I then had to maintain that drive and fear and motivation over a prolonged period of time. Ultimately, the drive and focus, along with a lot of work with a lot of great clients and lawyers, led me to build what became the second-largest practice at a billion-dollar law firm. I maintained that practice leadership as a group manager and a top rainmaker at the firm over a period of fifteen-plus years. A great number of the clients and lawyers who were part of that effort are still at the firm, leading and thriving.

We will talk in later chapters about the leader's role. Among other things, we will discuss why a leader ought to be judged in part by how well they develop other leaders and how well the company thrives after they are no longer there to lead. Great leaders build businesses and teams that excel after they are gone.

PASSION AND MOTIVATION

One of the funny things that happens in business is that fear and nervous energy often become gamified and fun over time. For me, it definitely evolved into embracing challenges with a sense of gamification. I vividly remember understanding what different growth numbers might mean and watching them constantly as I built my practice. The analyst at the law firm in charge of collection numbers by client got to know me very, very well. I loved reviewing and checking those numbers. *Loved it.*

I'll share some figures from that time, but remember that this was a long time ago—I really got going with practice-building in the mid-1990s—so the numbers might seem scant if you don't account for inflation.

When I started, I had two numbers in mind. The first was $300,000 in legal revenues. This amount of legal business, I thought, would provide me the freedom to stay or to leave the firm and either open my own practice or switch firms. By my estimation, $300,000 would give me a portable business, so I couldn't be held hostage by the firm if I wasn't treated properly or couldn't get the help I needed to serve my clients well. That number would give me autonomy, freedom, and options. To be clear, $300,000 was a number I calculated prior to having a family; costs and expenses tend to grow with life over time. (But that's a whole different story.)

The second number I had in mind was $1 million in legal revenues. Back then, at our 140-lawyer firm, there weren't very many people that had a book of business that large. Maybe ten to fifteen lawyers had more than a million dollars in business, and a handful controlled multiple millions. I perceived that $1 million in legal revenues would give me even more autonomy and, dare I say, "make me a player" at the law firm.

But such numbers, which are inevitably a little arbitrary, often don't have the impact you thought they would. The *pursuit* of numbers and *how you feel when you get there* are two different things. Goals work best as motivational tools, not as ends unto themselves. In any event, while I thought I would be a player at $1 million, I was quickly disabused of that notion.

My practice, when I got serious about it, grew in increments. My clients generated $7,000 in revenues the first year. That's the actual number, not a typo: My clients, the ones that I originated and brought into the firm, only generated $7,000 in revenues the year I started trying to build a practice. They grew to $50,000 the second year, $200,000 the third year, then $600,000, and $1 million-plus. Over time, they grew from $10 million to $15 million in legal revenues. This was before the inflation of the last twenty-plus years, so those were real and hard-won numbers. None of them came easy. It took spark and passion.

STARTING FROM ZERO

When you first start to generate some revenues, but the numbers are small, you can take one of two approaches: be encouraged and take your progress as fuel to grow on, or assume it's not worth the effort. I was fortunate to become obsessed with the effort. I viewed modest numbers ticking upward as positive encouragement. I then doubled and tripled down on my efforts and devotion to building the legal practice.

Your early numbers—and I think this is applicable to most startups—are often nothing in terms of real dollars. But, in my experience, the flip side was that few other young lawyers were at all focused on building a business or practice. A few small wins went a long way in giving me encouragement that I could be successful. I kept going.

Meanwhile, a lot of my competition settled for less. I have seen way too many people take the scant gains of their first years the wrong way. They essentially decide that they can't make their own success, so they go back to (in the law world) being solely a client-service lawyer. Don't get me wrong, just "having a job" versus leading a business or practice can be a fantastic choice . . . as long as it is *your* choice and *your* goal.

However, if you want to grow a business, it's highly likely that the first few years will be filled with small wins, small numbers, and a good deal of doubt. Most startups need to work really hard for a period of time before they start to get positive feedback. It's almost an act of faith, plus a little soothsaying, to keep going in the early days.

It's worth noting that if you are building a business while also maintaining your core job, you will, for all practical purposes, have two full-time jobs for a prolonged period of time. I'm generally a fan of the straddling approach as opposed to the burn-the-boats approach. But many people disagree with this. Both can be right and wrong. If you're listening to social media, you might believe that anyone who doesn't go all in on their startup, quit their day job, and burn the boats is somehow a loser. The reality is most of us need to pay the bills while we are building our business, and we need to keep the day job to do so.

For serial entrepreneurs, it's very hard to do this over and over again—to start back at zero and relive those early and middle years. Many entrepreneurs who are very successful at one business believe they are preordained to be successful in another. This is not my experience.

A successful serial entrepreneur needs to remember that you almost always need to get started again at zero. This is a hard, hard lesson to keep repeating. Many successful founders think they should be able to skip forward and avoid the early, challenging days of starting a business. That's like taking years to master French, then believing you'll be fluent in Mandarin in two months. In my experience, few of these founders become successful serial entrepreneurs. A serial entrepreneur needs to get back to loving the gritty, low-revenue days of a startup and to taking encouragement from the small wins.

Satya Nadella, the longtime CEO of Microsoft, captures this idea really well in his book *Hit Refresh*: "Success can cause people to unlearn the habits that made them successful in the first place."[6] This is a reminder that early wins can easily lead to complacency.

My second effort at seriously building a business came with the creation of Becker's Healthcare. The media company was built less out of fear and more out of seeing an opportunity and doubling and tripling down on it. This was an endeavor that took tremendous effort, focus, and drive.

The real energy and obsession with Becker's Healthcare evolved within me over time. I had been focused on building the legal practice for several years. I had built a great team and a great client base at the law firm. This allowed me to gradually turn the motor toward building the media business. It wasn't as though a switch was flipped; rather, I gradually became taken by the effort.

For most entrepreneurs, the insane desire to grow and build will come and go over the course of a lifetime. When I talk about that drive in building the law practice, I think about constantly monitoring what clients were brought into the firm, traveling and speaking to try to meet new clients, building an internal team, having constant status check-ins with those teams, and so much more. For nearly a decade, I lived, breathed, and ate building the practice. The incredible drive that I had then is not something most of us find all the time throughout life. Today, I often have a hard time duplicating the energy that allowed me to build the law practice and then the media firm.

One sign of how focused I had to be to grow the practice is the fact that thirty years later, I still remember those revenue numbers clearly—the first year at $7,000 and the fifth year at $1 million. I can say the same for some of our media initiatives. Our business and health-care podcasts have now been downloaded nearly 30 million times. In the first month, we had 143 downloads. Again, I had to start at the very beginning and embrace that. A lot of energy has to go into every effort.

SOURCING SPARK

The spark and motivation of an entrepreneur can come from multiple places. It might originate in nervous energy, it can come from sheer obsession, or it can be very thoughtful and methodical. Dave Thomas, the founder of Wendy's, often emphasized three fundamentals of starting a business: knowing your product better than anyone, knowing your customer, and having a burning desire to succeed.

Whatever your own motivation is, that motivation better be very deep . . . almost obsessive. Growing a startup business will require tremendous energy and focus over a sustained period of time. In essence, as Dave Thomas says, it will require a burning desire to succeed. I love this thought.

The flip side is that you will almost certainly need to make some serious sacrifices. For example, for me, over a long period of time there were no guys' nights out and very few other activities. Time-consuming hobbies, like golf or trips with the buddies? I missed all of those. Essentially, there was business and family.

That said, I did use various tricks to maintain sanity and energy. I started very early in the morning, but I made it home for dinner every night, unless I was away on business travel. The cell phone was kept off fully at night (this was a long time ago, so the phone was a Blackberry). I also always took a day off each weekend. If you want to grow something substantial, you will likely have to stay deeply motivated over a prolonged period of time—including when the business is showing very slow progress. You will also need to incorporate some regular rest and recovery.

There are pluses and minuses to this level of intensity, and that includes sacrifices. I would not have it any other way, and I think most entrepreneurs would agree. Most successful entrepreneurs realize you can't have it all at the same time. There will be seasons of life when you need to be very focused on building out a business.

Grant Cardone has a great quote on the drive needed to meet goals—and in this case, start a business—in his book *The 10X Rule: The Only Difference Between Success and Failure*: "Everyone knows how important it is to set goals; however, most people fail to do so because they underestimate the amount of action necessary to accomplish that goal."[7]

One of my favorite concepts (and all-time favorite song lyrics) comes from a Kenny Rogers hit that says, "You've got to know when to hold 'em, know when to fold 'em, know when to walk away, know when to run."[8] This is from "The Gambler." I've also heard someone say you need to know when to turn the lights out. You need to walk away, fold them, and turn the lights out when you don't have the passion and drive to make the business go—i.e., when you are no longer obsessed.

The thing about sparks is that they can ignite other flames. Your obsession is contagious, and a good leader knows how to use that fact to their advantage. Jack Welch, legendary leader and longtime CEO of General Electric, said this about passion and leadership: "The world will belong to passionate, driven leaders—people who not only have enormous energy but who can energize those whom they lead."[9]

CHAPTER 4

Launching Our First Healthcare Conference

Today, Becker's Healthcare hosts several conferences a year. These include health system conferences, a health system CEO and CFO conference, a payor summit, ambulatory surgery center conferences, orthopedic and spine events, health technology conferences, and a handful of others, both live and virtual. The Becker's Health Annual Meeting now draws several thousand attendees each spring.

A Becker's Healthcare conference includes several thousand attendees, several hundred speakers, and keynote speakers that include former US presidents and A-list celebrities. A recent conference of ours featured President George W. Bush, Olympic swimmer Michael Phelps, and tennis champion Venus Williams. Other conferences have included President Bill Clinton,

Secretary of State Hillary Clinton, NBA legend Kareem Abdul-Jabbar, and many other well-known celebrities. A recent CEO/CFO conference featured golf icon Jack Nicklaus, hockey great Wayne Gretzky, and basketball sensation Caitlin Clark.

This was not the case thirty-plus years ago. Our very first conference was in the specific area of ambulatory surgery centers. We held the conference at a Chicago-area airport hotel over one day. There were definitely no US presidents in the room.

There are a few things worth mentioning about this very small start. First, the motivation to start the conference was my desire to be in the middle of the surgery center area to build a legal practice. Second, I felt compelled to build the conference because a core method of reaching the business audience that I needed to reach was cut off to me.

The best way to meet the surgery center audience was through the main trade association that served surgery centers. At that time, it was called FASA—the Federated Ambulatory Surgery Association. Today, it's known as ASCA, and it's a great organization with great leadership.

Back in the day, FASA and its conferences were closely controlled by a team of leaders that included the law firm that worked with the trade association. Because of that control, I couldn't for the life of me get speaking spots or other opportunities to be in front of the FASA audience. This was an important audience for me because it included surgery center owners, physicians, and administrators. These leaders and their surgery centers were the target clients for the legal practice I was building.

Because I was blocked from speaking at the FASA conferences, I decided to start the first Becker's Ambulatory Surgery Centers (ASC) Conference. I was hyper-motivated to start the conference due to my being boxed out by the other law firm. What began as that single conference eventually grew into a company that hosted numerous events and, over time, expanded into other areas under the broader name Becker's Healthcare.

The company was first incorporated as FMW (MW were the initials of the competing law firm's name; you can guess what the F stood for). Over the years, the lawyers who drove those efforts at the trade association and the competing law firm each became close colleagues of mine. In any event, being blocked out early on fueled my motivation and purpose in starting our first conference. Again, at the time, it was an effort aimed at placing me in the middle of the surgery center business. I was trying to build a network, build visibility as a speaker, and brand myself as a leader.

I self-funded all the expenses of the conference and the entire business for nearly twenty-five years. (We will discuss the funding of startup businesses later on.) I also used an outside conference-management firm to run many aspects of the conference. They did a terrific job, and I worked with them for years, until I got serious about really growing the business and building an internal team at what became Becker's Healthcare.

THE SLYWOTZKY APPROACH

While developing the conference, I learned some business-building concepts through a book by consultant and author Adrian Slywotzky, *The Art of Profitability*.[10] I recommend this book as a great business primer. Slywotzky takes the reader through several business models and discusses the concept of being the switchboard, or the central connector, in a given area. I love his writing.

There are seven takeaways worth noting here.

1. Side projects can become serious businesses. When I started the surgery center conferences, I didn't really think I was launching a business. I saw it as a vehicle to build thought leadership and market my legal practice—not as a standalone venture. Over time, my eyes opened to the possibility that this could be a real business in itself. A few years into the conference and newsletter efforts of Becker's Healthcare, I realized that I could try to turn it into a serious company.

2. Much of success stems from spotting opportunities. So much of life, business, and career success is doing what you are doing and keeping your eyes open to opportunities. When you see them, you need to double and triple down. As Jim Collins says in *Good to Great*, "Pour the coals into the efforts that are showing promise."

We advise people in their careers or their businesses to spend 80 percent or more of their time and energy on their core business and about 20 percent of their time exploring new ideas and opportunities, reading, and networking. Focus first on what your core job is and second on trying to connect the dots and develop new opportunities. I find that people who spend 80 percent of their time looking for the next job or opportunity are rarely successful. There are exceptions to this, but by and large I believe you need to always try and excel first at the core job you already have. Do that job well, try to connect the dots, and then find and pursue opportunities adjacent to that core or that emerge as you attend to it.

3. Pay attention to your drive. When the drive hits you to grow something and to invest your time more fully into the effort, don't ignore that voice. For most of us, passion and real drive hit periodically, not all the time. When it hits and you feel it, go after it.

4. Early on, outsource broadly so you can learn and grow. With startups, I am a huge believer in outsourcing whatever you can outsource until you are ready to build internally and really try to grow your business from the inside out. Aside from the many benefits of good outsourcing partners, this can also allow you to test ideas for a business without taking on too many full-time employees and too much risk. You can also utilize outside partners who are great at a specific area you need to dig into without having to build a team around it.

We will discuss outsourcing extensively later on in the book. Then and now, my core principle is to outsource everything you can and to bring your most critical departments and areas in-house. For example, at Becker's Healthcare we built internal sales, editorial, conference, data, and key account teams, but we have largely continued to outsource multiple other areas of work.

5. Pay attention to signals of fit. To fill up that first conference with attendees and speakers, I spent a lot of time talking to people and trying to convince them to join. It wasn't that hard to get people to come, but this is not always the case. There are some spots where gargantuan efforts can lead to small results. If the efforts are huge compared to the payoff, you may not be finding product-market fit, or you may be approaching it wrong. The fact that I could get people to come to the early conferences helped me recognize that there was some real interest in what I was doing.

6. Ideas often happen when you are doing the work. It is very hard to abstractly develop business ideas. It's much easier for some of us to see them when we are engaged in the business and the work. This is another reason I encourage aspiring entrepreneurs to stay highly focused on their core job and profession.

A great quote on this last concept comes from Paul Graham, co-founder of seed capital firm Y Combinator: "The way to get startup ideas is not to try to think of startup ideas. It's to look for problems, preferably problems you have yourself."[11]

It is very hard to "whiteboard" startup ideas. It is much easier to see them while you are engaging in business. That being said, you do need a disciplined plan to sit down periodically and think about the ideas you are collecting and evaluate them as business opportunities.

7. Many great businesses have started when other doors closed. I remember early in my career working with a group of doctors led by Paul Summerside, MD, and Bruce Bressler, MD. These two physicians started a hospital after Dr. Summerside's emergency medicine group was cut out from working at the local hospital. The same local hospital also tried to hire their own neurosurgeons. That drove the doctors to plan a competing hospital so they would have a place to work and some control over their futures. This was an almost unheard-of concept at the time. It reflected tremendous drive, spark, and determination.

Dr. Summerside also helped open another golf club in his town when he and his colleagues were unable to become members of the existing club. I love that. This kind of motivation—to build a business, club, charity, or anything substantial—can be difficult to manufacture. Some people, whether driven by a chip on their shoulder or by innate ambition, seem uniquely able to channel that energy and push forward with remarkable drive.

But drive is only part of the story. There's often a need for risk as well. Let's talk about how to know when (or if) to take the plunge and go all in on your business.

CHAPTER 5

Should You Burn the Boats and Quit Your Day Job?

There is so much written on social media and elsewhere about whether you should quit your day job, or "burn the boats." In essence, do you quit your steady gig and thus force yourself to go all in on your business with no backup plan or safety net? The idea is that the leap will force tremendous drive and motivation.

The quote "burn the boats" is originally attributed to Hernán Cortés, the Spanish conquistador who ordered his men to destroy their ships upon arriving in Mexico in 1519. By removing any path of retreat, Cortés ensured that his army had no option but to move forward and fight to win.[12] This metaphor, like many sports and military metaphors, can be inspiring . . . but can also be an imperfect comparison for business.

Should you burn the boats and go all in on your business? This is rarely a simple yes or no question.

Personally, and for several reasons, I never quit my day job as a lawyer at the firm. I built the media business side by side with the day job. This is certainly not the answer for everyone, and it certainly stretched me greatly at times. However, it fit my financial situation and my aversion to too much risk.

In the early years, this meant that at the law firm I helped take care of clients *and* worked at marketing and bringing in business. Trying to serve clients extremely well and in a very hands-on way while also trying to build a serious practice felt like two full-time jobs. Later on, I continued to work on maintaining and building the law practice while simultaneously getting the media company really going. This again felt like two full-time jobs.

I didn't quit my job for several different, though sometimes overlapping, reasons. First, I simply didn't have the income to live on without it. This was the case for the first several years. Second, I used the income from the legal job to fund the growth of the media business. Third, I loved the law firm. I loved growing clients and teams in the firm, and I really enjoyed working with a great number of my colleagues. For a long period of time, growing the legal practice remained my primary passion and business. Fourth, the entire second business—the media company—was initially started *to help grow the legal job*!

LESSONS

A few lessons came out of my situation.

First and foremost, I could not have done this without building great teams in both the law firm and the media company. We will return to the concept of building teams. I believe—and you will hear a lot about this—that building teams of great, talented people is absolutely fundamental to building successful businesses.

But the more complicated question about boat burning is this: Could you do better in one business or the other if you fully focus on only one? Personally, I don't know that I would have performed better in either if I had just done one or the other. This is because, in both businesses, I was fortunate to have the equivalent of CEOs who were better at that job and at running the business than I was. I believe that if I had been fully immersed in both businesses—if I had stayed involved in every aspect instead of concentrating on the parts of business-building I did best—I would have driven those leaders crazy and been as much an impediment as an asset. I might not have built the great company, practice, and teams that I ended up developing.

Ultimately, I don't know the answer to the one-or-the-other question. Analysts could argue both sides. In my case, I believe the dual-track approach worked best. But for most people, there likely comes a point in time when it makes sense to choose one business or job over the other—to burn the first boat. However, I have seen many people fail in business when they took this path too early. They had to spend years thereafter trying to financially and professionally recover. They burned the boats back to job number 1, but the business they were starting ultimately failed. This is a bad outcome.

The large majority of startup businesses fail, usually in their first year. This is why a huge number of great businesses are launched by entrepreneurs who keep their core job until they can safely devote themselves fully to the new business.

Again, I don't have an absolute thesis on this; I just know what I did and what worked for me. But I do believe that once you are past the sink-or-swim phase, most businesses would do better if they made a different choice than the one I made. In the end, timing is everything.

Gary Keller is a brilliant thinker and author who wrote a book called *The ONE Thing: The Surprisingly Simple Truth Behind Extraordinary Results*.[13] I love his thinking. Here is one of my favorite quotes from the book: "I looked back at my success and failures and discovered an interesting pattern. Where I'd had huge success, I had narrowed my concentration to one thing, and where my success varied, my focus had too."

I think his advice is largely right on. I too may have had greater success if I'd religiously followed this guidance. Then again, maybe not. For whatever reason, I've often found myself deeply involved in two serious—and sometimes overlapping—business pursuits at once. Professional consultants would no doubt argue that I would have been better off focusing entirely on one effort rather than splitting my time between two. Ultimately, I'm not certain they'd be right. For most leaders and entrepreneurs, there's a constant battle for balance: the balance between what may be optimal from a strictly business standpoint and what best fuels that person's internal engine. It's important to know yourself and what gives you drive. Without that, all is for naught.

Product-Market Fit

The most successful businesses serve a real customer need. They are built at the intersection of what a business and founder are great at and what the market or customer really wants. Many businesses are founded around their founders' passions or ideas, but this is only one part of the game. Ultimately, you need both: something the founder and team are great at and want to do, and something the target customer really wants and needs.

Jeff Bezos, founder of Amazon, has a great quote on customer needs that translates well into product-market fit. "We are not competitor obsessed, we're customer obsessed. We start with what the customer needs and we work backward."[14]

There is no business without product-market fit. I often say, somewhat jokingly, that when a company has invested a ton of effort but has no revenues and no customers to show for it, the founder really has a hobby—not a business.

FROM FUNNEL TO FIT

We view business as a funnel of five phases:

1. Idea
2. Product
3. Customers and Revenue
4. Profit
5. Scale

A huge number of businesses never get to the third stage—customers and revenue. This is often because they have not spent enough time in stages one and two—idea and product development, which is about talking to potential customers about whether they want the product or not.

Michael Dell, founder, chairman, and CEO of Dell Technologies, has a great quote on this: "Ideas are a commodity. Execution of them is not."[15] I have seen failure in this area so many times, when founders build a solution that the market doesn't want or need. As a founder, I have been guilty of this myself, and I assume many other founders have been too. Here are six thoughts on testing and finding product-market fit.

1. Every team and founder must commercialize early.

You need to speak to customers and potential customers just as you are getting going or even before you get started.

One of the most brilliant businesspeople I know has built multiple massively successful companies. He once said to me, "We don't fund a business without having our first customer signed up." Similarly, a real estate developer won't build a project without presales or precommitted leases. You can't build a surgery center without first signing up surgeons.

You may not need to go as far as these three examples, but in any business, you will need to talk to customers as early as possible to assure there is a real market for what you're doing.

Another one of my favorite concepts—which I relate to finding product-market fit early—comes from one of my all-time favorite song lyrics: "Nobody rides for free." If a lot of people you talk to like your idea, but no one will actually buy the product or pay for it, then you are likely lacking product-market fit. I use the phrase "nobody rides for free" to describe customers who say they love your project but don't want to pay for it. I try to disabuse them of that notion . . . particularly if they are obnoxious or pushy about it.

2. Many engineers build businesses or software solutions but fail to talk to customers early.

One firm that I mistakenly invested in ultimately went broke because it never found its market and its product-market fit.

3. In talking to customers early, you want to think like Reid Hoffman, Jessica Cole, and Jim Collins.

Reid Hoffman says to get out to the market as soon as possible with a minimum viable product. Jessica Cole and Jim Collins emphasize testing—firing bullets—and figuring out quickly if the market wants what you're selling.

Several oft-mentioned concepts are super important here. For one, perfection is very much the enemy of the good. You need to try and talk to customers and potential customers early and get real-world market feedback. And you need to try and sell to them early to see if they really want to buy or if they are just nice to talk to. You cannot wait until your product is perfect to introduce it and try to sell it.

The reality of any great business is that you will never be done building the product or service. Hence, you need to commercialize early, and you must commit to "constant improvement." Test the market, get going with the minimum viable product, and commit to a lifetime of improvement.

Apple, Epic, Microsoft, and Intuitive are great examples of constantly committing to improvement. Customers do business with these companies in part because they know they are always trying to get better. Apple is on its seventeenth release of its iPhone. Last year Intuitive released the Da Vinci 5, its latest iteration of its flagship surgical robot.

4. Spend time early on trying to define and home in on your ideal customer.

This customer can, and should, evolve over time. But any business that doesn't know its target customer and target market is likely destined for subpar results or failure.

5. A market pivot usually reflects a missed shot at product-market fit.

When a well-funded business comes back to its board to say it's making a big market pivot, it often leads me as an investor to think I'm destined to see my investment come to zero. Yes, pivots of some sort are always going to be needed. But when a company says it's making a market pivot or an industry pivot, it almost always signals to an investor that they missed the boat on product-market fit on their early market and product efforts.

Again, you don't have a business without customers who are willing to buy what you are selling. Without customers, you have a hobby.

Some founders are so brilliant they can see and understand a market and the potential for a product. Most of us, myself included, are incrementalists: we need to constantly test the market and constantly try to improve.

6. Lasting success comes from differentiation.

I love this quote from entrepreneur and investor Peter Thiel: "All happy companies are different: each one earns a monopoly by solving a unique problem. All failed companies are the same: they failed to escape competition."[16] This inversion of Tolstoy's famous opening to *Anna Karenina* is an education in itself. The lesson is that success is as much about the market as it is about the idea.

CHAPTER 7

Small and Medium-Sized Clients Are Often the Starting Point

When I started to build the legal practice and then the media company, I had to learn many different concepts and lessons fairly quickly. You learn a lot of these lessons through direct experience rather than reading or hearing about them. Sadly, many of us have to learn them through trial and error and through hard work.

In those businesses—and I think largely in any business—you quickly learn terms such as *sales cycle* and get a feel for how long the sales cycles are for larger potential customers. You learn concepts like *ideal customer profile* and many others. Over time, these ideas help you better understand who to target, how to approach them, and how to build a more effective sales strategy.

When first building a business, you learn firsthand that clients of a certain size have a very quick sales cycle and that larger clients have a longer process. The small clients may meet you and hire your firm with little bureaucracy—often on the same day or the same week that you first pitch them. The larger clients often have many sub-processes and decision points, and they can take months to years to decide to buy from you. Anyone who has sold to a health system or any other large company realizes that the sales cycle can be very extensive indeed.

Whether building a legal practice or building a media business, I saw firsthand that smaller companies would commit to doing business with us very quickly, while larger customers were far harder to land. This lesson was equally relevant in building the law practice and the media business. Most every entrepreneur or sales professional comes to understand this basic truth intuitively over time.

Most businesses (there are always exceptions) will start with small and mid-sized customers and then grow into acquiring and servicing larger clients. It's important as a business developer to understand this and to have a regular thought process in place as to how to build an organization that, over time, can serve larger customers. It's very hard in business-to-business arenas to build a serious enterprise without targeting medium-sized to large clients. You will often *start* with small clients to get the business going, but you have to plan to grow into serving larger and larger clients over time.

Smaller clients can be a pleasure to work with, and you can develop very close relationships with them. They can also be very appreciative. However, smaller clients may have a hard time bearing the rates you must charge to grow an organization and build an elite team. Thus, if you want to scale a larger business over time, you will need to grow into acquiring and serving larger customers who have bigger needs and bigger spending potential.

ANCHOR CLIENTS

When first building my healthcare legal practice, the initial clients I was able to bring into the firm were often individual ambulatory surgery centers and individual practices. The leaders of those practices or centers could often make a hiring decision in no time at all. This was very helpful to both getting some numbers on the board and gaining confidence that we could be successful.

But make no mistake, in the long run, it's very hard to sustain and build a great business around small customers. There can be exceptions. For example, a software firm that targets thousands of small customers can excel with every customer paying a relatively small subscription fee per year. However, even there, the business probably needs anchor or core customers to retain its target numbers.

We often used the term *anchor clients* or *core clients* to describe the type of customers who would do a certain amount of business with us. For example (and this will differ in every business), an anchor client might spend $1 million or more a year with your company; a core client might spend $100,000 a year or more. The small and mid-sized clients that you started the business with may spend significantly less than that.

As we grew our legal practice, our team of lawyers, and our skill sets, we started to pinpoint the type of client we would target for business more thoughtfully. A single practice or single ambulatory surgery center was what we called a Tier 4 client. We could still serve them very well, but they didn't always provide regular, ongoing business of a significant amount, though they might offer a big deal or big piece of litigation periodically.

A large practice or larger facility might be a Tier 3 client—one that would have ongoing needs requiring more help.

An individual hospital or chain of surgery centers might be a Tier 2 client.

A large healthcare company, a larger chain of surgery centers, a large health system, or a private equity fund that invested in healthcare might be a Tier 1 client. This type of Tier 1 or 2 client would have ongoing needs for services of a significant magnitude. Our goal was to try and work very closely with these clients as an extension of their team. These anchor or core clients would help us keep the lights on.

As you grow your team and your business acumen and develop a book of clients, you are often far better able to attract the larger ones. You are also more likely to have a portfolio of small and mid-sized clients that will allow you to keep the business going while pursuing larger clients with longer sales cycles.

Barbara Corcoran, real estate mogul and investor, often emphasizes the importance of stepping beyond your comfort zone. Her advice highlights how taking on clients—including smaller ones—outside of your expertise fosters essential learning and business growth. As she puts it, "Don't be afraid to go for positions, jobs or take on clients just outside of your knowledge base. It's when you're uncomfortable that you can learn and grow the most."[17]

LARGER DEMANDS

As a business pursues larger clients, it's worth noting that the demands on your team and talent will also increase. Larger clients are likely to have more complex needs, and they can often be more demanding.

The flip side is that as you grow a business, very small clients can present their own challenges, especially in terms of their ability to pay the amount it costs to grow and retain your team. We used to joke that a small client would want you to work twenty hours and want to pay you for five. Smaller clients can also require more hand-holding, as their business can be very personal to them.

We had a similar experience when building Becker's Healthcare. Many of our original clients were smaller companies that wanted to exhibit at our early conferences and paid very small amounts to do so. At one time, a Tier 1 sponsor might spend $5,000 a year with us. That number over the years moved upward to more than $1 million per year for an anchor client.

DEVELOP CAPABILITIES TO SCALE

Some firms are deeply funded from the beginning. For example, Peter Thiel and his team built Palantir Technologies to serve governments and large customers. However, even there, I would bet that many of their first sales were to smaller customers.

As your efforts become more sophisticated, you can better deliver what mid-sized and large clients need. In developing and moving from small to large clients, four key lessons come to mind.

1. You need to take care of your customers very well. The worst thing you can do in most businesses is churn through clients. Ultimately, you want recurring clients, not turnover. At every business I'm part of, we very closely track the retention of our customers. Adding customers is important, but great businesses really thrive by retaining great customers and delivering results for them.

2. Bigger clients require bigger capabilities. As your business grows into larger clients, you will need to make sure you have the right, talented people to serve more complex and demanding customers. A customer that spends $1 million a year with you will require more in almost every way than one that spends $25,000. Your capabilities and ability to deliver great services will need to constantly evolve and improve.

3. Most firms reach another level when aligned with clients that match their strengths. The relationship with clients in your sweet spot can help both you and the clients thrive. The best clients get billed fairly and are reasonable about the discounts they demand. Most importantly, you and your best customers act as partners in growing together.

4. Avoid fragility. You want to avoid a situation in which you are reliant on a few customers, leaving those customers in a position to cause tremendous stress to your team and your finances. Part of growing is diversifying your client base, not through churn but through growth. Multiple regular customers is the ideal.

Scaling a business is as much about discipline as ambition. It requires serving customers exceptionally well, building the capabilities to handle more complex demands, and aligning with clients whose needs fit your strengths. Equally important is maintaining balance—growing without becoming dependent on a few large customers. When you develop the right mix of people, processes, and partners, you not only earn bigger clients but also build a stronger, more resilient company for the long term.

CHAPTER 8

Point Solutions vs. Broader Solutions

A great majority of businesses will start by offering what are known as *point solutions*. However, most will ultimately need to move beyond that.

Point solutions are products or services designed to address a specific problem or function within a larger system. Many businesses start by providing a point solution, such as a specific software application that solves a very specific problem for a customer. The company providing the point solution likely specializes deeply in that area and may be much better at solving that problem than a bigger company that offers many products and services.

A great example of starting with a point solution is a company called LeanTaaS, which built a software solution that helped hospitals manage operating room logistics. It became the best company at solving this very specific problem for hospitals and health systems. Similarly, the aforementioned company Intuitive has (for nearly thirty years!) focused almost exclusively on building robotic surgery platforms. LeanTaas and Intuitive have expanded greatly and grown into world wide leaders in their niches and in adjacent areas.

This aligns with another powerful insight from Paul Graham of Y Combinator, who posits that the best products don't try to do everything; they focus on solving a single problem better than anyone else.

"When you demo, don't run through a catalog of features," he writes. "Instead start with the problem you're solving, and then show how your product solves it."[18]

Another example of a point-solution model might be a revenue cycle management firm that handles just one part of the revenue cycle. In contrast, some revenue cycle firms provide what are called end-to-end solutions. A revenue cycle firm might focus only on health systems or physician practices. It's similar in law. Some law firms may make the effort to specialize solely in surgery center transactions rather than provide a wide variety of services for surgery centers. In media, a company might solely offer podcasts or webinars as a means to reach its audience. In our media business, we at Becker's focus on several niche areas within healthcare and provide our customers the ability to reach their customers in those areas through a variety of means.

MAKE IT EASY FOR THE CLIENT

If offering a point solution in a very specific area, there must be a big enough market to build a viable business around that point solution, and you need to be so good at that solution that companies want to hire you. Your company also has to be so easy to integrate into workflow that customers will be eager to work with you. No one wants to work with too many vendors or with vendors who aren't easy to integrate. A great point solution must excel at what it does—and be easy to integrate into the customer's business.

We recently worked with a writer who solely does one kind of writing. This is great if that kind of writing is all you need; you can work with others on the other aspects of a project. However, this model fails when a vendor's limitations encumber your workflow.

In the building world, you can hire a great architect or a great builder—each is a point-solution business. A design-build firm takes the opposite approach, combining design, architecture, and construction under one roof. Companies like Airoom do this intentionally, taking on more complexity, infrastructure, and upfront investment in exchange for deeper relationships and larger, more comprehensive projects.

I have tried to build a media company or two around highly specific point solutions. Generally, I struggled with them. I found that clients didn't want just that point solution or that others offered the same solution in a better way.

As another example from the media world, a medical device company selling to surgery centers might reach its audience by simply exhibiting at our conferences or advertising in our newsletters. Each method is a point solution. But when we needed multiple solutions for customers to really reach and engage their prospective customers, we decided to offer a broader array of products focused on both lead generation and branding. This meant developing a mix of point solutions: conferences, newsletters, websites, white papers, webinars, and more. It worked.

STARTING SMALL VS. STAYING SMALL

I would guess that most great small businesses begin with a very specific point solution for a very specific area. Those businesses are often so good at helping customers solve that point solution that they do it better than much larger companies. But, as we will discuss later, most companies that start with a niche or a point solution will eventually need to expand beyond that initial point. Both LeanTaaS and Intuitive built great businesses in areas where customers had deep needs and big problems to solve. As I mentioned, LeanTaaS built a strong business with technology and software for surgical operating room management and later expanded into other types of procedure room management. Intuitive began with surgical robotics and, through continual enhancements and wraparound services, has largely remained focused on that space. Intuitive has consistently improved both its robotics and its overall offerings within that niche.

This discussion may lead you to think that building a business that is the very best in a very discrete area is the way to go. Unfortunately, it's not that easy. This may be the best way to start a company, but most businesses need to go beyond the point solution in the long term.

Epic is the most popular electronic health records software for hospitals and health systems. But Epic also tries to handle many other items for hospitals as part of or as an add-on to their EHR enterprise solutions. In healthcare, many smaller companies set out to solve very specific needs and problems for hospitals and health systems. Epic, as a healthcare tech giant with seemingly endless resources, has solutions for the same problems these smaller companies target, but Epic's solution or module to one problem or another may not be as good as a smaller company's dedicated point solution. The small tech company has to be so good at what they do that the health system doesn't default to Epic, which may include the tool at no additional cost as part of its overall system.

This scenario can teach us a few lessons.

First, customers increasingly want to limit the number of suppliers or providers they work with. They rarely prefer a thousand different point solutions, each with its own vendor. Even if the point solutions are considered best in class, clients don't want to manage too many different vendor relationships, contracts, and ongoing maintenance tasks. If invoicing weren't a problem, integration would be. Hospitals and health systems are constantly trying to reduce the number of technology point solutions and vendors that they work with. That's good news for companies like Epic.

Second, large companies also try to cull the number of vendors they work with. GE, back when it was one of the most respected companies in the world, would constantly try and refine the number of suppliers on their books. As Ben Thompson, founder of Stratechery, has argued, point solutions can win early, but over time they either integrate into broader platforms or get competed away by them.[19]

Third, companies that invest in your firm want to have multiple areas they can grow into. Soon we will come to a discussion about how to fund growing businesses. That includes some important thoughts on outside funding at different points of the business journey. Where you are in your business's path to success makes all the difference. That's why it's important to remember advice Eric Ries, author of *The Lean Startup*, has long emphasized: Start by solving a specific problem for a specific group, then use that foothold to grow.[20] Ries's quote emphasizes an important concept: a great point solution is often a starting point to get into a market—not the end point in building a business.

Finally, from a company perspective, you need to have large enough revenue and size to hire and build great teams. This is often very hard to do with a discrete point solution unless the point solution solves a big problem in a substantial area.

Customers might not want just one single way to solve their problems or reach their audience. They might want to choose which way to do it and via which solution. Your job in building a better business is to be the best, easiest solution. That's how you get their attention. How you keep it will come down to you.

CHAPTER 9

Reference and High-Impact Customers

In any business you build, there will be key early and high-impact customers. Those early, important customers take a while to develop into close clients. But, over time, these high-value clients become what I have already referred to as core or anchor customers. These clients keep the lights on and are hugely important as a reference for other potential customers.

One rule I live by regarding high-impact clients is a similar rule I give to young professionals in building their careers: It's much more important to be highly valuable to a handful of great clients than it is to be a little bit valuable to a lot of come-and-go customers.

Most great business-to-business firms are built around a small percentage of customers that are disproportionately important to the company. It is a central job of company leadership to know which clients and types of clients are the most important and to make sure the company is taking care of those customers extremely well. In short, your best people and efforts should be focused largely on the customers who spend the most money with your company, because these key clients offer a lot more than cash flow. Here are a few hard and fast reasons why.

RESPECTED EARLY CLIENTS GIVE YOUR BUSINESS CREDIBILITY AND OPEN DOORS.

There is a type of customer who is highly respected in your business area. Signing them is important because it signals to other current and potential customers that your company is worth working with.

One of our early clients in the initial stages of building a surgery center–focused law practice was a company called Ambulatory Surgical Centers of America. The leader of that firm was a doctor-turned-entrepreneur named Brent Lambert, MD. Brent was a bigger-than-life personality who was brilliant, funny, and hugely well respected. When he and his team started to grow with us and trust us with their legal work, it was the greatest endorsement we could have ever had. It gave us a whole different level of credibility.

We had a very similar experience when we became the principal outside law firm for two surgery center chains, Regent Surgical Health and Physicians Endoscopy. These relationships greatly enhanced our reputation. They were a clear signal to other potential customers that we knew what we were doing.

Over time, we developed great reference clients and practices in the health system area and then in the healthcare private equity area. Every reference helped, especially when the client was respected in their field.

DEEP RELATIONSHIPS WITH HIGH-VALUE CLIENTS CAN FUEL YOUR GROWTH.

In addition to keeping an eye out for reference accounts and understanding their impact and importance to your client list, it's critical to understand the overall impact of high-value clients on your internal recruitment.

Early on, you need some clients who do enough work with your business that you can recruit, hire, and retain the talent you need to build the business you want to build. At both the law firm and the media business, we had enough clients who were willing to work with us that we could afford to keep investing and growing the business by growing our team. Some of our foundational early recruits came to us because of the reputation of our early client list.

YOUR CLIENTS ARE YOUR TEACHERS— YOU LEARN BY DOING.

In almost any business, your clients learn from you. But it's just as important that you learn from your clients.

When I did my first surgery center sale transaction for a client in Ohio, I learned a huge amount about the surgery center transaction business. By the second and then tenth transactions, I had a great deal of valuable knowledge compared to others when it came to how the business worked and how deals got done.

At your starting point, you and your business are rookies. Over time, you become truly knowledgeable.

A great take on reference customers is put forth by Marty Cagan, the founder of Silicon Valley Product Group: "Let's be clear about what it means to be a reference customer: This is a real customer (not friends or family), that is running your product in production (not a trial or prototype), that has paid real money for the product (it wasn't given away to entice them to use it), and most important, they are willing to tell others how much they love your product (voluntarily and sincerely)."[21]

Reference and high-value clients—and staying very close to them—can have an outsized impact on the success of your firm. Business is not a democracy, and a key goal of leadership is to make sure that disproportionate effort is spent taking care of your most important clients.

THE BEST CLIENTS TREAT YOU LIKE A PARTNER.

Another note that I will add here is the concept of clients treating you like a partner versus treating you like a vendor. As you develop a client or customer base—in whatever business you're in—you will find over time that certain clients treat you as partners. They respect that you are in business too, and they take a genuine interest in your firm thriving along with them. This concept of a thrive-thrive relationship is critical in many business situations and relationships.

Other clients will treat you as a commodity vendor, "the help."

It's completely appropriate that each type of client will want a fair price for what you do for them. And they should get a fair price. However, there will be customers that treat you and your team in a very transactional and vendor-like manner. These clients over time can be profitable, but those client relationships are a lot less satisfying and often less stable. Invest your best in the partners.

STAY CLOSE TO YOUR ANCHOR CLIENTS.

Some core goals with your top anchor and reference customers are to stay very close to them, to try and always look to add extra value for them, and to anticipate their needs.

Back in the day, I was very fortunate to serve on the boards of directors of a handful of our clients. Today, it's generally uncommon to serve on the boards of clients. Twenty or thirty years ago, however, this was quite common—especially among small and mid-sized companies. At the time, this was a sign that they truly viewed us as a trusted advisor to them and their business.

KNOWING WHICH CLIENTS *NOT* TO WORK WITH IS JUST AS IMPORTANT.

In addition to knowing which clients are the most important, it's critical to know which clients you don't want to have as customers. These can be clients that treat your team poorly, clients that are outside of your niche areas, or clients that are too low value or simply not profitable. Again, business is not a democracy. You have to decide who you are going to work with and who you are not going to work with. Author and speaker Kevin Ward has emphasized that not every buyer is your customer—and that clarity about who you are not serving is essential to growth.[22]

A long time ago, we did a customer study and broke our customers into five quintiles. These were broken down by how much money the customers spent with us.

A small number of customers generated 20 percent of our revenues. They spent the most, on average. The second group was larger in number but spent less on average, generating the next 20 percent of revenues. (As an interesting side note, we found that the second quintile of customers was on average more profitable than our first quintile because our largest customers in the first quintile received the most discounts.) The same trend continued until we got to the fifth quintile. This one amounted to a very large number of customers that spent very small amounts with the company on average.

Several things were true about the last quintile: We couldn't make a profit on these clients, they took up a lot of time and resources, they often wanted large discounts, and they were frequently difficult to work with. Ultimately, the company decided we could no longer work with clients that didn't spend more than a certain amount of dollars per year or per project. The minimum amount a customer must spend with you to be a valuable or viable customer will likely increase as the company grows.

Don't be afraid to stop taking work if it's draining your energy, time, or morale . . . especially if it isn't even generating a profit!

CHAPTER 10

Niche-Driven Businesses

One of the great debates in business—and in many other aspects of life—revolves around whether it is better to be a big fish in a small pond or a small fish in a much larger one. I am typically a fan of trying to be a big fish in a small pond. This correlates with another great debate: whether your company should specialize or take on all kinds of industries and customers. Again, I'm generally a believer in specialization.

Someone recently asked me if it's better to go broader or to niche down. My unequivocal advice is to niche down but to test various niches. More on this later.

In business (and in investing in startups and growth companies), you regularly hear the term *total addressable market* or TAM. One of the old jokes in business and investing is the founder who pitches business plans around incredibly huge total addressable markets. Investors laugh. Presenting a business plan with a very broad addressable market often shows naïveté and makes investors perceive a company as less investable, not more.

A widely used example of this approach would be someone addressing their target market as "China" or "every consumer in the US." Any real investor immediately dismisses such thinking and the founder who floats it. Businesses must know what market they are trying to serve in terms of their ideal target customer. As author and entrepreneur Seth Godin puts it, "Find a niche, not a nation."[23]

There are a couple of good starting points in developing a target or niche market.

A first foundational assessment is whether you and your team are building a business-to-business firm or a business-to-consumer firm. I have some experience in advising companies in the business-to-consumer area. The main thing I know is that you need a great distribution system as much as you need a great product or service. Other than watching a few failures up front and personally, I don't know much else about business-to-consumer. The vast majority of my experience (and all of my success) has come in the business-to-business area.

NICHES

I have ultimately arrived at a couple of overriding thoughts on building businesses around niches. Many of these were solidified through watching others build businesses and through reading and following GE's Jack Welch.

I often think about niches with two questions to start: First, can you win in the niche? Second, is it worth winning in?

As you start to direct your business and your energy, you have to address the first question. Can you win in this niche? Generally, you don't want to start in areas that attract the most well-funded and aggressive competitors. This often means you will instead be building a small to mid-sized business in relatively less competitive areas.

When picking areas, I always found it super helpful to assess whether we could identify the key competitors. Even if there were just a few core competitors, did we think we could compete well with them? For me, the early core competitor in the healthcare law area was a firm named McDermott Will & Emery. The early core competitors in the healthcare media space were *Modern Healthcare* (for the health system audience) and *Outpatient Surgery Magazine* (for the surgery center audience).

When I first started practicing law, I worked in the corporate and securities group of a large, highly competitive firm. As I tried to build a practice, it became clear that the most lucrative areas—major litigation and large corporate mergers and acquisitions—were already dominated by elite lawyers from the top schools and firms, all competing with the sharpest elbows for the same work.

Could I have built a practice there over time? Possibly. But it was a brutal playing field, and success would have required outlasting people who were better positioned, better resourced, and far more entrenched than I was.

As to the second question, was it an area that was worth winning in? That was easy; it most certainly was. So, the rewards could be great, but the chances of winning were middling at best.

In evaluating how to position the practice and business that I was trying to build, I realized I was exhausted both from competing at the large law firm against the smartest lawyers and from working an insane number of hours to succeed. At some point, I started to look at other options for building a practice and growing as a lawyer.

By chance, I started to pick up some business from small and mid-sized healthcare clients. These were small pieces of business that weren't material at a large firm; they were clients that the largest and most prestigious and competitive firms were not trying to pick up or develop as clients. But those small wins started to help me see some signals.

Peter Drucker was one of the best management thinkers of the last hundred years. As to focusing all your efforts into very specific areas, Drucker writes in *The Effective Executive*: "Concentration is the key to economic results. No other principle of effectiveness is violated as constantly today as the basic principle of concentration . . . Our motto seems to be: 'Let's do a little bit of everything.'"[24]

Drucker also posits that one of the most important things a company can do is say no to everything outside of its core areas: "The executive who wants to be effective and who wants his organization to be effective polices himself to say 'no' to the marginal. He says 'yes' only to the few activities that make a difference."[25]

LESSONS LEARNED

In building the law practice and the media business, I learned so many lessons about positioning and niches. To name a few important ones:

1. Small, niche clients are very excited to hire someone focused specifically on their area.

2. Every larger client has some competitive firm that is jealously trying to protect that relationship. When you are pursuing larger clients, you should understand that the competition will always be far more intense than when pursuing smaller clients. For every larger client, there is some firm or company to whom that client is very important. The larger the customer, the more established competitors you'll face. It is much easier to bring on a small regional bank than it is to win JPMorgan Chase.

3. If you have to work too hard to find business in an area, you may be focusing on the wrong area. Here again, I like to be able to clearly define the core competitors in any business I'm in.

4. Defining your niche requires a mix of research, testing, and lived experience. In trying to define the niche business to target, there is a great balance between analyzing and researching potential markets and businesses, testing different areas, and seeing different opportunities from one's own experience and market knowledge. The right way to try and define markets and niche areas is probably a mix of all of these.

GET YOUR HANDS DIRTY

Some people can assess markets and options without being deeply involved in them. Personally, I find it much easier to assess from the point of direct involvement and to test areas with some outreach and effort. I have found it very hard to simply whiteboard or abstractly define markets without having a chance to actually be involved in those markets. I have often doubled down on niche areas after testing a handful. I then deeply pursue the ones that show the most promise and early positive results.

Generally, I am trying to target markets where there is not incredible competition from the largest companies. For example, I would not look to start a streaming network—I wouldn't want to compete with Amazon, Netflix, or Disney.

Another quote on niche markets that I like comes from venture capital investor Richard Koch: "Choose the niche that you enjoy, where you can excel and stand a chance of becoming an acknowledged leader."[26] Koch is a business strategist who also popularized the 80/20 or Pareto Principle: 80 percent of outcomes often come from 20 percent of efforts. By focusing heavily on a niche, your benefits can be outsized compared to the work.

My business efforts have always started with more attackable, smaller niches where the competition was not so stiff. As discussed earlier, when first starting to build a law practice and then a media business, I largely focused on ambulatory surgery centers. The biggest and most competitive firms, both in law and in media, were not targeting those areas, which left a lot of opportunity for growth.

A client in the surgery center space back in the day might generate legal fees of $10,000 to $30,000 a year on average. The client would generate more when it had a deal or litigation to process. In contrast, health systems and larger clients would generate far more than that in fees but were much more difficult to obtain as clients.

A good stable of small to mid-sized clients that you can serve well in a definable niche is a great place to start building—particularly if those customers can provide recurring and regular business.

Another huge benefit to building around a niche is that you start to develop expertise in that niche and a deep understanding of what those specific customers need. This can happen over a relatively short period of time, and it allows you to remain focused on your marketing and development efforts. You don't need to study everything, and you don't need to attend everything. Rather, you and your team can focus your efforts within the niche you are devoted to. This has so many financial and efficiency benefits.

Drucker spoke to this very well when he talked about concentrating all your team's energy into specific efforts and abandoning other areas that could distract. Koch's 80/20 rule applies here as well. Research has shown that the most productive companies—those that manage time, talent, and energy effectively—achieve profit margins 30 to 50 percent higher than industry peers.[27]

We talked about whiteboarding and starting to define areas to attack. I definitely did some early whiteboarding as I tried to find a niche to focus on. However, I encourage people to find the balance fairly early between whiteboarding and actually testing (i.e., trying to sell into an area). In general, I find many would-be entrepreneurs become too comfortable in the thinking stage and don't move quickly enough into the selling stage.

One of the best speakers on this concept is my longtime partner and the CEO of Becker's Healthcare, Jessica Cole, whose foreword kicked off this book. She urges business leaders to act and to be "ready, aim, fire" versus "ready, aim, aim, aim, aim, aim—and then fire."

In trying to assess niches to focus on, I believe there is not a silver bullet . . . if there is, I've never found it without a lot of testing and actual work in the niche itself. Generally, I preach against too much whiteboarding and too much thinking; I lean toward a lot of testing and signal-watching.

I had a senior partner at the law firm who built a thriving legal practice around a specialty area in healthcare. He became the preeminent lawyer in the country for nephrologists and dialysis facilities. He spoke constantly at dialysis and nephrology events and worked hard to stay closely connected to that specialty and its trade associations. His efforts were highly concentrated . . . and he was a very good lawyer. This combination allowed him to build an exceptionally successful practice in that field.

This success led me to consider similar areas and to look at and test niches. In this stage, I didn't just attack the surgery center area. Rather, I tested a practice in three distinct areas of healthcare: cardiology, disease management, and surgery centers. As I started to write, speak, and develop legal business in these areas, I found some success in all three. However, way more opportunities and business kept coming out of the surgery center area. This led me to really focus on the surgery center niche and double down there. Nothing succeeds like success.

FINDING YOUR NICHE

One of my core rules, as you know, is that business is not a democracy. When something is working well—be it people or niches or routines—I strongly believe in heavily investing effort and resources there. Study what is working for your business and double down.

There has been a huge amount written on how to find the right niche and why finding the right niche is so important. There are a few ways to go about this: First, you can do a good deal of studying potential niches. Second, you can dive in and test market reception in various areas.

My sense is that the right answer is somewhere between the two. I tend to start with back-of-an-envelope assessments of niches. Often, and to my inevitable regret, I suffer from not doing enough studying of opportunities up front. When making larger investments in an area, you would likely benefit from more research *and then* more hustle. More fully stated, I have had success in building niche businesses but would have been well advised to do more in-depth assessments in some situations before diving in headfirst. It can be very easy and very frustrating to jump into a niche and spend years in a rabbit hole chasing that niche without great success. I've done that. You lose a lot of sleep. In contrast, I have done much better when I both followed some signals and did some testing.

A great example of following the signals happened at the law firm with a practice in the dental and dental services organization area. As a team, we were constantly assessing where clients were coming in from and how much work those clients were doing with us. As we got going, we would strategically spend most of our time marketing into the areas that we were building in—for example, the surgery center space.

But as we made progress in growing a practice and a platform, clients would also come to us from other areas both in and out of healthcare. At one point, a dental practice management chain was referred to us, and they were on a great growth trajectory. They began using us for all their legal work and started to spend several hundred thousand dollars a year with the firm. As we observed this and followed the numbers, we built a specific initiative around the dental practice management area. This is an example of following a signal and then investing in that area.

You have to stay nimble and responsive if you want to capitalize on opportunities. Part of that agility requires humility when it comes to planning and foreknowledge. It means learning to distinguish between what you think you know and what you actually know—and then making decisions based on that distinction.

You ought to have some ideas about areas you want to go into. When exploring a new area, I am a huge fan of testing and commercializing early. Reid Hoffman, co-founder of LinkedIn, has a great take on this: "If you are not embarrassed by the first version of your product, you've launched too late."[28] I encourage all founders to commercialize and test early. In contrast, I see some engineering teams build software for a niche or area they think wants that software only to discover that the market is not so excited for it.

Failure is inevitable sometimes; that's why it's so important to watch the tea leaves and concentrate your energy on what's working. *Double and triple down on the successful niche.*

NEW HORIZONS

Adjacent markets often present the next best move. As you start to look for additional niches to grow into, one popular concept is to view the initial niche as long-term or semipermanent. I generally agree with this concept. Ideally, there is enough business and opportunity in the niche to grow a serious business and to hire and retain great people around that area.

Many businesses hop from area to area; I view this as a bad strategy. We are trying to build long-term, solid businesses—not make a quick buck in area after area. That means you have to take each additional niche as seriously as you took the first. When you assess additional niches to grow into, look both strategically and opportunistically.

From a strategic perspective, I am a huge proponent of a concept explored in depth (and brilliantly) in a book called *Profit from the Core: A Return to Growth in Turbulent Times.* The book speaks both to the concept of digging deeper into your core areas and about growing businesses adjacent to that core. In summary, you will find much more powerful synergies when you branch out and attack areas adjacent to your strengths. I love this advice and tend to succeed when I follow it.

In both the law business and the media business, we religiously and aggressively followed the concepts set forth in *Profit from the Core.* In law, we used the surgery center business as an entry point to other adjacent and related areas. We went from individual surgery center clients to larger and larger chains of surgery centers. We also started to develop business in the health system arena and in other specialty areas in healthcare.

Originally, many of our health system clients hired us to help them with projects in the surgery center area. This is one of the benefits of being so strong in one niche; people hire you or work with you for that lead area and then expand the work you do for them into other niches or categories. This type of win-win is most likely with those ideal clients who see you as a partner rather than a vendor.

We saw this play out repeatedly. As hospitals began developing joint-venture surgery centers, they hired us for that work, then increasingly relied on us for a broader range of services and transactions. Over time, those relationships became core, anchor partnerships. We saw the same pattern with private equity firms investing in healthcare—what began as narrowly scoped engagements grew into long-term relationships as our role expanded alongside their businesses.

In addition to developing areas that were targeted as adjacent to our initial niche, we also started to grow other niches in an opportunistic way. As I mentioned, when we started to have dental practice management firms hire the law firm and spend serious money with us, we recognized the opportunity. One of our partners took the lead in developing that area as a line of business.

Another great quote from *Profit from the Core*: "The key to sustained and profitable growth is to find a repeatable formula that utilizes the most powerful and differentiated strengths in your core and applies them to a series of new 'adjacent' markets."[29] A company should leverage its core strengths to expand into adjacent markets in a strategic and repeatable way.

The story of expansion and growth in the media business closely resembles the growth of the legal practice. The media business began with a singular focus on surgery centers. (Note that this was itself a kind of adjacent expansion of the law practice.) It started with a simple newsletter and a small conference. The company was very focused on building an audience of the surgeons who worked and invested in surgery centers and the administrators who helped to manage and run surgery centers. The audience also included companies that managed and invested in surgery centers. Our money was made through companies that wanted to meet that target audience. They would advertise in the newsletter and exhibit at our conferences.

From there, we began to build a little business in this niche area. We did a great deal of work to maintain the right audience-to-exhibitor balance at the conferences. Conferences remain attractive to both vendors and attendees as long as you have the right ratio of audience to exhibitors. In contrast, I saw another competitor's conference grow less attractive and ultimately fail when they started to have too many vendors compared to attendees.

SCALING

As you start to grow a business, certain things almost inevitably lead you to reach a certain amount of scale. Many times, this need for scale is far less about making more money and far more about building a sustainable team. Many of these lessons I learned firsthand while building the legal practice.

When the legal practice first got going, I had one young associate lawyer working essentially exclusively with my clients. If each lawyer could generate at that time—and it's a long time ago—$200,000 to $400,000 in legal fees, then between me and the other lawyer we could have enough business to make a nice living, plus our freedom at and from the firm. Basically, it would be enough business that if the firm treated us poorly, we could leave. (As an aside, the firm has been great. After thirty-plus years, I'm still involved with McGuireWoods.)

Here is the big lesson I learned: If you have a one-person team, you are completely at risk of that person leaving. Now, this person who worked for me was an outstanding young man. Eventually he took a job at a much larger firm, making more money. Good for him . . . but it left me high and dry. It was a very stark lesson: You cannot be too dependent on any single person. Instead, a sturdy business needs to be large enough to build a sturdy team. We will talk extensively in chapter 11 about teams, talent, and more. We will also discuss customer concentration, ride-or-die people, and single points of failure. All these lessons came at me directly from the school of hard knocks when the other lawyer left.

As always, the lesson was the silver lining. Being too at risk of losing my only team member instilled the clarity that I needed to try and build a larger practice and, later, a larger media company. In the late 1990s, the media company started to hire people full-time. Soon I had a handful of full-time employees. In part because it was a startup team and in part because I was working full-time in the law practice, it became clear to me that we needed to become a slightly larger business to be able to attract and retain the right people. This led to the need for expansion.

Paradoxically, when building a bigger business, your core goal is often not to make more money but to gain more depth and become less fragile. These two purposes can overlap, but they don't have to. For example, you may need to build a bigger team or make investments simply to protect your profits.

We decided to grow, and to do that we needed to double down on our core business of surgery centers while also expanding into other markets. Again, we took those first steps at the media business nearly twenty-five years ago. I didn't do deep analysis or deep business plans for the new areas. Instead, I identified a couple of areas close to our core, and we had conversations among ourselves and with a handful of our top customers. Then we tested the waters and waded into two adjacent areas: orthopedics and health systems.

When they are very, very engaged in their business and watching it closely, great managers and leaders can have insights that come to them clear as day. Back in the day, we and our leadership teams at both the firm and the media business were so close to the businesses that it was easy to spot opportunities. We almost always knew we would do fine in the areas we moved into. Then it was more of a question of whether the new area would be adequate, modestly successful, or very successful—a single, a double, or a home run. This is one of the huge benefits of being close to your business, building close to your core, and not having to abstractly whiteboard for new ideas. Stay fully engaged and ready to connect the dots. As I often say, "Grind, yes—but grind and think."

A special thank-you in our expansion efforts goes to one of our early customers, VMG Health, and specifically to Greg Koonsman. As we assessed new niches on the back of the envelope, this firm looked at our new expansion areas and was immediately supportive. I vividly recall being at an airport and reaching out to ten or so customers about expansion into 1. orthopedics and spine and 2. hospitals and health systems. A few customers, like VMG Health, just responded with, "We're in." That was very meaningful.

Each time we added an area, a handful of our customers were willing to be early sponsors and help us grow the business into that new area. These early words of encouragement and the early financial support through advertising in these areas were really meaningful to us.

In business, a small number of relationships make an outsized impact on your longtime success. It's not thousands of relationships; it's more like five to twenty that make a huge difference. This is true in business and in life. A key skill as an entrepreneur is recognizing when these people and firms enter your orbit, seeing the possibilities, and doubling or tripling down on those relationships.

When we got going in orthopedics and spine and in hospitals and health systems, the media company had a simple playbook: We would develop a newsletter in these areas as well as a print magazine (this was a long time ago) and hold a small conference. It was a simple game plan. We tried to make sure we had two events per year for each niche.

We also started trying to find advertisers for the new areas. We began with our running customer list and tried to assess who also wanted to reach those new markets. This is one of the beauties of growing into areas adjacent to your core. You often already have a base of customers along with a base of know-how and expertise. At the same time, we'd begin building lists of prospective customers who actively advertised to these markets.

THREE KEY LESSONS ON NICHES AND EXPANDING

As we started building a business in the orthopedic and spine market and with hospital systems and health systems, we learned three great lessons.

1. Expect surprises when entering adjacent markets. First, when you start in an adjacent market, you will almost always begin with some expectations and biases. For us, we thought we would really thrive in the orthopedics and spine area because it was so closely adjacent to the surgery center market. Many owners of surgery centers were orthopedic groups and orthopedic surgeons—the same with spine surgeons and spine-focused groups. This goes back to the question of whether you can win in a given market.

On one hand, we were right: We did very well in that market. We were very focused on orthopedics and spine, and we were able to quickly develop an audience in this area and then a number of advertisers who wanted to reach that audience. Thus, we received positive feedback and built a viable and profitable niche business very quickly.

On the other hand, there were real limits to growth in that niche. The largest advertisers—major medical device companies—built direct financial relationships with surgeons, bypassing media companies altogether. As a result, they had little need for media or conference outreach, which made a company like ours increasingly dispensable.

Furthermore, the trade organizations for the orthopedic and spine areas had deep, deep loyalty and strong influence. For example, the American Academy of Orthopedic Surgeons did—and still does—an incredible job serving the orthopedic surgeon market and attracting a large, engaged audience. That's stiff competition.

2. Great markets are not just winnable—they're worth winning.
The highest-growth area for our media company turned out to be hospitals and health systems. That growth helped

crystallize my thinking around the second key question we've discussed: Is it an area worth winning in?

We started to win. We had one great competitor. We focused heavily on digital because they were so strong in print. We had no choice; we could not afford to compete in print. We still did tremendously well, as did they.

Aside from the win of doing well, we really learned the lesson about what markets are worth winning in. The health system market was a much larger and more lucrative market than orthopedics and spine. To our team's credit, we kept following the signals and doubled and tripled down on that area.

3. Be number one or two or get out. Former GE CEO Jack Welch had this business philosophy: "A business that isn't number one or number two in its market has no place in our future."[30] We took this to mean that if you are first or second in a market, you thrive in good times and you survive through tougher times. We adopted this concept and loved it. I carry it with me to this day.

CONCLUSION

Business success rarely comes from chasing everything. It comes from knowing where you can win and committing to it. The most enduring companies learn to define their playing field clearly. They pick a niche, master it, and expand only when it makes strategic sense.

At the same time, niches aren't static. As markets evolve, so must the businesses that serve them. The challenge is to stay close enough to your core to draw strength from it while remaining alert to adjacent opportunities. This balance is where real growth happens.

Ultimately, building a niche-driven business is an act of discipline. It's about understanding your strengths, serving your customers exceptionally well, and saying no to distractions that dilute focus. When done right, a niche becomes more than a market segment—it becomes your company's identity, reason for being, and competitive advantage.

CHAPTER 11

Teams

This is one of the most important chapters in the book. In this chapter, I will weave in the story of building Becker's Healthcare and the healthcare law practice with lots of lessons and observations on building teams. I'll share some background from each business and ten or so lessons I have learned through these experiences. Grab your highlighter.

Two early influences revolutionized my thinking on building teams. They each entered my life a long time ago and solidified my thinking on the building of teams as perhaps the most important factor in business success.

First, when I was a young lawyer, I sought the advice of a lawyer named Gerald (Jerry) Peters at a firm called Latham. Jerry was a pioneer in building a healthcare legal practice. He was based on the West Coast and generously took the time to sit down with me and talk about practice building. He told me that the key to his incredible success was assembling a talented team. It was a shocking admission, and it really stuck with me.

Second, I read work by two authors who talked about building teams. Their thinking also struck a chord. Jim Collins writes in *Good to Great* that the most important key to success is getting the right people on the bus. Garry Keller in *The One Thing* speaks on how the single-most important thing he had to do at his company was get the right people into the right leadership spots. Read those books.

THE MYTH OF THE SOLOPRENEUR

But before we dig into teams, I want to discuss the concept—or, as I like to say, the *myth*—of the "solopreneur." The concept of the solo entrepreneur is talked about often on social media. It's the idea that one can build a serious business by themself.

I have tried going it alone, and I have tried building a business with partners and teams. Personally, I have found time and time again that it's incredibly difficult to build anything serious as a solopreneur. Sure, one can build a solo business that can pay your bills so you can make a living. However, whether you outsource key parts of the business or hire people full- or part-time, my sense is that it's nearly impossible to do anything sub-stantial without building teams.

Yes, the teams you build can be outsourced. But even when outsourcing a great deal of a business, most serious businesses will need some full-time people every day to really build and scale. The great entrepreneurs in our country are iconic; the not-so-secret truth is that they all built very serious teams. Between Steve Jobs, Bill Gates, Elon Musk, and Judy Faulkner, none of them did it as solopreneurs.

Seth Godin challenges the myth of the solopreneur—the idea of the solo hero—arguing that while going it alone can sound admirable, it often leaves founders isolated and limits what they can build. Paul Jarvis, author of *Company of One* and a co-founder of Fathom Analytics, argues that solopreneurship concentrates both the upside and the strain: You keep the wins, but you also absorb the workload and the risk of burnout.[31]

Most can't sustain the pace of solopreneurship over a long period of time. Thus, if acting as a solopreneur, fully dependent on yourself, you'd best save a lot of money . . . because at some point you will need to slow down. When that day comes, you won't be able to earn like you did.

This really hit home when I began to build a team in the law practice. The team allowed me to take care of clients while also having the time to try to bring in new ones. At Becker's Healthcare, the business did fine for the first several years, when I outsourced everything. But it really grew when I started to hire full-time employees and build a team. Many of those teammates ended up being extraordinary. More on that later.

You can be a solo business as a consultant, writer, executive coach, or many other things. But my sense is that if you want to build something large, you likely have to commit to building teams. People can run great but limited consulting services or similar businesses by themselves. For example, the therapist and the executive coach who I speak to from time to time each have great solo practices. They are brilliant. But those solo businesses can't grow into bigger businesses unless they choose to build teams. Every dollar they make comes from an hour they put in. This is very hard to scale.

Building something big will require a team. The team can be outsourced, or it can be internal. My personal experience is that in almost all situations, there is no way around ultimately having a core, largely full-time internal team. That team can be leveraged with lots of external resources.

TEAM BUILDING AT BECKER'S HEALTHCARE

I have tried to build businesses through teams, and I have tried to build businesses without teams. All my successes have come when I made the effort to cultivate and build a team, and all my failures have come when I have been too lazy or didn't want to spend the money. For me, this is a no-brainer.

At Becker's Healthcare, I spent the first five to ten years outsourcing essentially every part of the business to a conference-management firm. They did a great job.

At some point, I started to see great potential in the business, and I wanted to try and build it into something bigger. I had an aha moment after reading an article about famous entrepreneur Sheldon Adelson. He made his first fortune building and then selling the Consumer Electronics Show (now known as CES) for nearly $1 billion. This was like a lightbulb going on, telling me that my thought-leadership effort to build my legal practice could become a full-fledged media business of its own. I was building a business with some real potential.

At this point, my core goals and visions were different from those of the conference-management team I was outsourcing. They were working with me and with several other companies and had limited interest in sustainably growing the business. But I was starting to get obsessed and excited about growth.

I tried to maintain work with my outsourcing partner *and* hire a couple of people. The outsourcing partner did not like this. They decided to terminate our partnership. At that point, I learned a great lesson in fragility. I was fragile, and I found myself scrambling to make the business work.

Thus, I had a choice: find a firm to replace the management company or double down on my efforts to build a team. I chose to build the team. Thank God we weren't that big then. I didn't need to hire many people to manage the small business we had. The company was still small enough (and I still had enough energy) to work through this transition and keep things going as I built a team. It was a stressful period. You have to limit single points of failure, and you have to limit reliance on any one supplier. Firms that are too reliant on any one supplier often learn this lesson the hard way. You can avoid both of those perils by building deep enough teams to limit business fragility.

The separation with my outsourcing partner led me to hire a handful of initial employees. It was a very diverse group made up of various people I knew from different places. One was a former writer at *Modern Healthcare*, one was a great former paralegal who worked with me at the firm, and one was a young, smart early careerist who I knew from his efforts selling suits to lawyers. It ultimately worked out great, but randomly assembling a team was probably not *the* way to do it. It worked out . . . but I probably should have been more intentional.

I hired these people to help with sales and operations and conference management and more. Like I said, all of them were people I knew, but none of them had specific experience in what we were doing. When you hire like this, even if the people are solid, it requires a lot of hands-on management. As I have gained experience, my hiring thoughts and processes have become a lot more sophisticated and clear.

I have increasingly focused on hiring people who have achieved serious success in their current job or school, who haven't job-hopped, and who demonstrate a mix of diligence, drive, intelligence, and strong interpersonal skills. That said, I also strongly believe that every hire is an educated guess and that you don't truly know how well someone will fit until they've worked with you and your team for some time. Hiring is always a gamble.

While I was managing this group, a client leader named Tom Jacobs from a firm called MedHQ called me and asked if his niece, who was at the University of Iowa, could work with me for the summer or intern during college. As I often do—for better or worse—I essentially said, "Sure." I remember interviewing his niece, Jessica Cole. It was by phone from the Denver airport. I hired her on the spot. I figured I'd give her a shot, and I didn't really think anything more of it at the time.

By this point, I had nearly ten employees, all contributing in some way to the business. I was running the legal practice full-time as well. I was trying—though often failing—to keep the media company simple and manage it on the side, so I managed lightly and hoped for the best. I was running a relatively small business, but with nearly ten people on the payroll, it was getting challenging.

We had constant status and update calls with the team to make sure things were moving in the right direction. At that time, the media company operated as a fully remote team. Most things get done by phone and email these days, but this was before the heyday of remote work. There weren't tools like Slack, and even texting for business wasn't customary.

The intern, Jessica Cole, worked remotely from her apartment at the University of Iowa. She quickly began to outperform several full-time employees. And when I say outperform, I mean she was driving sales, organizing everything, and just doing an incredible job. No one else came close. She was running circles around the experienced adults I had hired.

By the time Jessica was age twenty-five or so, I threw up my hands and put her in charge of everything. She oversaw the entire team. She was extraordinary. About half the team quit, unable to believe I'd made this young upstart the leader of the entire organization. But it's all about the right talent and the right teams—and God, was I right and were they wrong. Jessica, our team, and I went on to build a much larger business and a much larger team over a long period of time. Fast-forward to today. Jessica still runs our relatively lean organization. We still outsource strategically to leverage the full-time team.

There is a key lesson here that I come back to time and time again: One of your core roles as a leader or a founder is to know who your best people are and to retain, embrace, and double down on them. And to keep doing this.

At the law firm, I had a very similar experience. To build a serious business and take care of clients, I needed to build a more expansive team. Early on, I would keep a team of one or two lawyers. Inevitably, one of those people would leave, and that was always very stressful. I used to gauge the impact of someone's departure with an imperfect but real scientific measurement: how bad a stomachache I got. I used to call this the Grikas Rule after one of my first great hires left the firm when I still had a very small team. (Grikas is and was an outstanding lawyer and person.) I remember each one of the early key people I was fully reliant on and who left for what they saw as greener pastures.

After having this experience a few times in the early years, I learned that I needed to build a bigger and less fragile team. At one point, we built that team into more than thirty-five lawyers working nearly full-time on clients that I had originated.

ELEVEN CORE LESSONS ON TEAMS

1. You don't know what you have in a hire until you work with them.

Some hires come in with tremendous promise; everyone has already anointed them the next great leader. More often than not, this is not the case. Other hires come in, and no one has high expectations, then those hires turn out to be super talented and motivated with a very high motor. They slowly—almost quietly—become incredibly important. The first lesson is don't overly prejudge your hires. Instead, assess their fit and talent over time.

2. Recognize great talent and get in front of it.

When you hire someone and they show themselves to be exceptional over a period of time, it is your job as a business builder to embrace them and double down on them before they find a reason not to be excited about the organization.

In my experience, this often meant finding them leadership opportunities, promotions, and raises before they asked for them or thought about them. It meant a lot of one-on-one discussions with them about their careers, what they wanted, and how to make the environment work for them to thrive. Whether at the law firm or the media firm, I constantly tried to double down on great people and embrace them. Again, a key job of the leader is knowing who your best people are and focusing a lot of attention on them.

When I saw that Jessica was a great leader, I wasted zero time in begging her to stay for the long run and paying her more than I could afford to. When you see great talent, embrace it.

We learned this lesson starkly at Becker's Healthcare and at the law firm. As I started to sort out talent in building a team, I would recognize great drive and talent and work to make sure they were excited to join us. At the firm, I started to build a cadre of incredible lawyers who were leaders as well. Many of these leaders remain with the firm today. They are amazing and too numerous to mention here.

3. Try to build teams and businesses with a "thrive-thrive" mindset.

We don't look for perfection—but we do look for greatness. We will talk later about compensation and loving your 90 percenters.

We want all of our people thriving and the organization thriving, side by side and together. Situations in which the organization (or leader) thrives while the team members are wrung out like sponges in a top-down way are not sustainable. I preach thrive-thrive leadership, where each person thrives, *and* the company thrives. I don't expect a perfect overlap between what the person needs to thrive and what the company needs to thrive. Rather, I view it like a Venn diagram where there is a large—but not perfect—overlap between their contributions and the firm's needs.

I remember an early boss we used to joke about: A penny for him was worth more than a dollar for anyone else. That's a terrible philosophy. Our view is simple: Both the person and the organization need to thrive, side by side.

4. One of the hardest challenges in starting a business is sorting out teams and sorting out people.

When you get going in most businesses, particularly if you are not a deeply experienced serial entrepreneur (though this is true even if you are), you will likely have a potentially messy group of people working with you. If you make the effort to sort those people out and recognize the leaders, the contributors, and those who shouldn't be there, you can set the foundation for long-term success. If you don't make the effort to sort these teams out, you are likely heading for a long-term stretch of mediocre or subpar business.

This sorting out of people means, in the first instance, that you decide who should be with you and who shouldn't. Most of this will reveal itself to you in a fairly short period of time if you are highly engaged with your team. Then it's important to appoint, manage, and align your team. In the early days of most businesses, the need to sort out and align a team will require an extraordinary number of regular huddles and team meetings. (One key trick is to keep these huddles quite short.) Then the founder or CEO has to sort out who should be with the company for the long run and who should be exited. Whenever I could, I would ask people that I wanted to exit to start looking for a job so they could interview while they still had one.

This sorting out of teams is one of the most important things a leader has to do.

Back in the day, GE used a concept called force ranking to weed out the bottom 10 percent of performers each year. They would divide people into three categories: A's (top 20 percent), B's (the middle 70 percent, solid performers), and C's (the bottom 10 percent). They would then remove the bottom 10 percent each year.[32] I don't believe you need to be this extreme. However, I believe that in the very first years of a startup, you will need to find people you want with you for the long run and move people out who don't belong.

While you may not need exact categories of A, B, and C players—and it may be unpopular to talk this way—most successful organizations need some metric for understanding who their top performers are, who the solid performers are, and who is not contributing enough. If you keep team members around who aren't helping, you lose the chance to hire new people who will. You are wasting money on compensation that would be more smartly allocated to better performers. Finally, too much latitude with underperformers also sets the wrong culture for the company.

This is difficult stuff, but it's essential.

5. Most companies should never stop hiring.

To keep building a great team, you need to keep adding team members. This doesn't mean you hire enough people to put the company at financial risk. Rather, try to constantly build capacity and cultivate a pipeline of talent.

My core philosophy has been to spend a lot of effort building a leadership pipeline within the organization: build juniors into seniors. Try supplementing that with lateral hires from time to time, as needed and to fill gaps. Due to both natural and desired attrition, most firms must keep recruiting.

Over the long run, we've had great luck in building juniors into seniors, and many of our very best people have been with us for nearly their entire careers. Many of them are today's leaders both at the law firm and at Becker's Healthcare.

6. The "one-third, one-third, and one-third" rule.

A typical staff breaks down like this: One-third of your employees are indispensable; you want them with you for the long run. One-third are really important contributors; they are very important to the company. The bottom one-third are below-average contributors; they are fairly replaceable. In great organizations, the percentages of people in groups one and two expand over time, and those groups become more and more the overwhelming percentage of your team. For example, the ratio might shift into something more like 30:50:20—and better and better.

You want the number of people who are fully replaceable (or below average) to become lower as a percentage of your team. Keep trying to improve overall quality. Great leaders and managers are highly attuned to who is doing the work and making the organization better and to who is not.

Overall, I would much rather hire a smaller number of people with all people being paid above market value than a larger team with people paid below or at market value. I like to build fairly lean teams. That way, I am never far removed from the customer or the staff, and I have great talent at every level.

7. Pay everybody.

In many companies, the company makes the mistake of overallocating compensation to some groups of performers versus other groups of performers. From my perspective, we need to compensate the people in categories one and two—great and good performers—really well. I also need to compensate the underperformers well enough that they can keep their jobs, not come to resent the company, and figure out if they want to become higher-level performers.

To take this discussion a bit further, if I overpay leaders but underpay juniors, then the work of those leaders gets harder and harder because they aren't working with great junior people. I'd rather everyone make a great living and have great people throughout. This philosophy—fairly lean teams in which everyone is getting paid well—has led us to thrive for thirty-plus years in both businesses with next to zero layoffs.

This doesn't mean that compensation is a democracy. Your very best people should be paid extremely well. Anyone who has actually run a business (not just commented on it from the sidelines) knows how valuable your best leaders and CEOs and ride-or-die people are. Pay them and treat them like your life and business depend on it.

Here is one key error I made on compensation. From time to time, during recessions or with college graduates needing a job, you can hire people really inexpensively, and the people are really thankful. However, I have found that if those people aren't making a good enough wage, even if they were unemployed previously, they leave quickly when they have opportunities. I call this the Gordon Rule. They may have asked for a below-market salary—I appreciated that, and it made it easy to hire them—but they couldn't live on the wage they were initially thrilled. Once they had a job and some confidence, they would leave for a higher-paid opportunity.

When people ask for compensation that is less than they need, it's usually a warning sign, not a bargain. Even if they're willing to accept it, underpaying someone creates instability and resentment over time. Never underpay— even if your people are willing to be underpaid.

That said, if you are going to overpay everyone, you also have to make sure you keep cultivating and building a team worth paying well.

As always in building teams, I'd much rather have a smaller group of great people making a good to great deal above market than two or three times as many people making market compensation or less. Over the years, I have watched lots of companies hire two to five times more people than I did—and become more fragile and less successful when it came to margins, growth, and profitability.

Many of the companies that aggressively staff up are often venture capital funded and periodically go through big layoffs. Some of this is by design. Some VC-funded firms are pushed to grow revenues and headcount as fast as they can to find a plateau. When they find that place where revenue growth becomes less rapid, they bring headcount in line with those revenues. I understand the plan and why they do it. It's just not how I prefer to run a business.

8. As you build businesses, you are going to develop "ride-or-die" team members—the people you want by your side throughout your entire career.

As a leader, your job is to recognize who your ride-or-die people are and to always treat them as such. Keep doubling down on them. I talk a lot about allocating your time to your best people, your best customers, and your best business lines. Allocating your time to your very best performers is one of the most important things a leader can do. I want to grow and retain ride-or-die people. I want to make sure they are thriving and secure, and I want to keep doubling down on them.

I recall one senior officer saying in a board meeting that we needed to be less reliant on a certain ride-or-die leader—that we should make her expendable. I told the officer he should let go of that thinking until I retire. He wasn't wrong, per se. I just vehemently disagreed with him. As we build great organizations, our first goal is to build up and keep our best people. I want them feeling secure that they are in the right spot with us.

Yes, you want to keep on building depth; I want ride-or-die people, and I also want to add more ride-or-die people. But your best people are probably even more important than your best customers. In both cases, you always want to think in terms of addition. Keep your best person and add more great people. Keep your best customers and add more great customers.

When you don't make your top people secure, and they leave as you hire more great people, three bad things happen: First, you don't gain because you haven't added more top talent. Second, you lose great people, and you don't really know if the new ones will be as excellent. Third, you have lost institutional memory. The lesson is to always think in terms of "and."

At my first law firm, a stated goal from the senior partner who I reported to was to make another person good at what I was doing as soon as I got good at it. For example, I learned how to do an antitrust filing called a

Hart-Scott-Rodino filing. This was fairly complex and had to be done on larger transactions. I had done a few of them on major deals and felt like, "Wow, I finally have some importance here—a reason for being and being needed." The senior partner on the team very bluntly said we needed more people who could do it ASAP.

Now, this is a bit complicated. Yes, he was totally right. In any organization, for anything important, you need to have some depth and redundancy. However, as you build some depth at your elite- and good-performer levels, you need to aggressively work to make sure your top performers feel highly valued. Again, the senior partner wasn't wrong, but the way it made me feel was . . . expendable.

This has shaped how I see leadership. I believe it's crucial to ensure that your best people know every day how much you value them—especially as the business and team grow. I ultimately left my first firm in part because I didn't feel valued there.

9. In addition to loving your ride-or-die people, you need to love your "90 percenters."

There are valuable team members who do 90 percent plus of what they need to do extremely well. These people are very important to your organization and need to be greatly appreciated. These people may not ever become your elite, ride-or-die folks. But they are a huge part of the core that companies are built around. When you have lots of turnover in this tier of people, things get much harder for the whole organization. In the hospital world, health systems lost huge numbers of mid-career nurses during COVID-19 and have had a hard time building depth since. This meant senior leaders were working extremely closely with newer hires who had very little experience. This is very time-consuming and hard on your top performers.

Time and time again, I have seen managers aggressively focus on the 3 percent to 10 percent of things that a person doesn't do great. My view is that this is horrible management; they ought to spend the huge majority of their time appreciating and focusing on what the person is doing well. In almost everything you do, you want to focus your attention and time on what is going great. Once I sense that a person is great but is not going to correct their imperfections, I am very cautious about spending any time berating them for those weaknesses. This is particularly true if they are doing a huge amount right and the weaknesses aren't fatal to their continued growth.

10. When you have great people, clear the way for them to stay with the company for the long run.

When one of our ride-or-die people had to take a job in a city where the firm didn't have an office, we fought and then changed firm policy to allow her to work remotely. This was twenty years ago, before remote work was a concept. This was a critical decision. That person ultimately ran the department and joined the firm's executive committee. We had similar experiences when people moved to Charlotte, Ohio, and elsewhere. Come hell or high water, I wanted to keep those great people.

Similarly, when someone who is proving to be a big performer is ready for a bigger role, you need to find them a bigger role at the company. If you do not, they will find a bigger role elsewhere.

11. If your intention is to develop long-term relationships with your very best people, recognize that they will have serious ups and downs in their careers and lives.

If you have great people and you are with them for a long time, there will be times when they aren't performing at their best. If those people are important to you and the organization, you need to be very patient and provide grace. Even great people will have ups and downs.

We had a great partner who lost his wife to illness. Of course, he couldn't operate at his best level for a period of time. Another lawyer moved to Ohio and had to wait to practice until she passed the Ohio bar exam. When people have shown themselves to be invaluable over a long period of time, you have to breathe and be patient. You also need to have sufficient enough capacity that you can work through these times when your great people aren't at their best. You need some capacity to allow some flexibility.

Nothing is more important to a founder than developing and investing time and money in building great teams. Those teams will come to define your business and your legacy as a leader. If you treat your best (and second-best) people as the treasures they are to your enterprise, you will establish a foundation that can support a business for your entire career.

CHAPTER 12

The Founder's Evolution

I fundamentally view the evolution of a founder—and a business—in three core stages. This evolution is obvious in most small to medium-sized startups, though it's often somewhat different for well-funded venture capital startups. But even in those cases, a lot of these concepts will resonate.

In the first phase of a startup, the founder largely does everything by himself or herself. He or she may handle sales, operations, and all other tasks, large and small. I remember negotiating with hotels, planning agendas, getting outside help with billing, writing the newsletter, depositing checks, and so much more. We love this concept called The Joy of the Bank Run. (Thank you to Justin Breen for bringing that idea into his book.) As a relatively young founder, I would take the checks—which were mailed in to our home address—and drive them to the bank to deposit. This brought me great joy:

Things were working, and clients were paying their bills! It also placed me squarely in the middle of a core function: cash flow. Cash flow remains king for most startups. Getting paid today, even though I gave up bank runs a long time ago, still provides a dopamine fix.

This is intended to help demonstrate how many menial things a founder does until he or she learns to delegate. For most businesses, there are no real shortcuts around the early stages of learning your business fully. When you try to avoid these learning stages—for example, by trying to delegate early—you run the risk of not getting to know your own business and value proposition.

We had a fantastic, outsourced sales firm in a later business I founded. The CEO of that company scolded me once . . . and he was right on. He essentially told me I needed to be on several of those early sales calls to understand what my prospects wanted.

"After you have done that and understand your product-market fit and your value proposition," he said, "then you can delegate and scale."

In other words, you first have to really know your own business. He was brilliant.

Entrepreneur and leader Elise Contarsy says it well about this early stage: "You can't manage what you can't see—turn every dial, pay every bill, know the details."[33]

A book by business author Jeffrey Fox called *How to Become a Rainmaker: The Rules for Getting and Keeping Customers and Clients*[34] speaks a lot about the role of the leader and founder and how deeply that person must be involved in small to medium-sized businesses in their early stages. I found it to be true: To really know our business and our clients, I had to be deeply involved in both the law practice and the media business for a serious period of time.

Fox also wrote *How to Become a Great Boss: The Rules for Getting and Keeping the Best Employees.*[35] I highly recommend both of Fox's common-sense, easy-to-read books.

In the second phase of being a founder, you start to hire people to do many of the things that you used to do. Like bank runs. These people are not necessarily better at the tasks than you are, but this first level of key hires helps leverage and free up the founder to do more to expand the business. The founder has more time to sell and more time to execute. Nonetheless, there are limits to growth in this phase of the business, as everyone is still largely working under the direction of the founder. Thus, the business is still limited by the founder's bandwidth and abilities.

The big difference between what I view as levels two and three in the evolution of the founder is the quality and depth of the people the founder is hiring. The third stage begins when the founder has built a team of leaders with stronger capabilities and greater depth. When done right, the leaders of the various departments can fulfill their roles in their areas better than the founder could. This is when the business can really grow. It's no longer constrained by the founder's vision, ability, and daily management.

At Becker's Healthcare, we grew to the point that each leader of every area was better at their job than I was when I did it. The CEO was better than me, the leader of key accounts was better than me, the editorial leader was better than me, and so on.

This can be challenging on the ego of the founder. At the same time, in my experience, it's the only real way to take a business to another level and have it really grow. I vividly remember discussions with some of our leaders when we got to stage three. I was still too prone to micromanage. One leader said to me, with what took some gumption on her part, "Do you want to come back and do this job?" This was incredibly clarifying. First, I realized that there was no way I could do the job as well as her. Second, I also realized that as much as my ego had taken a step downward, I didn't want to go back to that role. Third, I realized I had better learn to manage lightly and get out of the way.

To return to Gary Keller's *The One Thing* and tie it into the founder's evolution, a founder must determine the core mission of the business—what the business does, how it does it, and for whom. Who are its customers, what is it doing for those customers, and how is it doing it? Then, the founder or leader has to focus on assembling and aligning a great group of leaders and great teams accordingly. A great founder also has to know what the company doesn't do and what business it doesn't pursue.

A great reminder about building high-quality teams comes again from Jeffrey Fox: "7s hire 5s and 9s hire 10s."[36] His point is twofold. First, you want your managers to hire people who are more talented than they are. Second, you need to remind yourself as a leader to keep hiring for greatness—not just to fill seats.

If a firm is not careful, its leaders may hire less talented people than themselves to feel safe, because they are intimidated by more talented people. Sometimes your managers aren't smart enough to realize what greatness is. This can lead to a downward cycle of mediocrity.

In contrast, you want to constantly hire really talented people who are as good as or better than you. This is where organizations can grow and thrive and get to level three. That brings us to the next chapter and what we call stacking leaders and concentrating efforts.

CHAPTER 13

Stacking Leaders and Concentrating Company Efforts

As we grew our businesses and mapped out how people would be allocated to what efforts, I learned several lessons about stacking and concentrating.

A core function of leadership is to constantly stack your best resources around your best clients and best areas. You need to keep your teams highly aligned with one another and around the most important areas of business. For example, if one of your business lines generates 70 percent of your revenues or profits, you need to focus your best people and teams on that line. Similarly, you need to stack your best people and teams on your top 20 percent of customers. I had the philosophy that the least important thing for the most valuable customer was still the most important thing. In short, I wanted to concentrate a huge percentage of our time and effort on our top customers.

Several bad things can happen with a poorly planned surgery center. The worst-performing surgery centers often have a dozen different specialties doing a great number of different types of surgeries. In contrast, the most successful centers are focused around one to three specialties, and all their efforts are concentrated on being great in those specialties. In a high-performing center with two to three specialties, all recruitment, all training, and all buying are built and focused on the specialties.

In contrast, a center with many different specialties needs to buy equipment for multiple fields, train staff to work with multiple scenarios, and cater to a wide variety of patients and their needs. This is a recipe for subpar operations.

The same applies to your business. In whatever field you're in, you want to decide what your most important areas are, and you want to stack talent and resources around those. For example, in our media company, I don't want to try to be great in fifteen different areas. Rather, we have dozens of people in our key areas. The editorial team has dozens of writers, the sales team is deep and great and the conference and key account teams are stacked with great people. If we have an area or department comprised of just one or two people, we are likely to outsource that area.

In addition to stacking people around key areas, we also have a very clear sense that we want to constantly align our best people with our most important efforts. Our top lawyers and account managers in the respective businesses work with our most important clients. Period. If we have an opportunity to grow a client with serious potential, we always assign our best team to that effort. It's the same with new high-value areas.

I recall a young lawyer engaged in work for a very demanding client who generated small revenues and paid their bills slowly. This was a D or F client we probably should not have been working with. This lawyer became so pushed by this client that he would have to ignore the needs of one of our best clients. He was good. We had to reconcentrate his efforts on the top clients. This became a very clear lesson for me in how to operate a business.

Being disciplined about placing your best people in the company's most important areas and in the service of the most important customers is one of the best things you can do in your business. This is not always a popular concept among those who don't get tapped to lead those efforts. It can be very hard to explain to a solid performer that the best client opportunities and growth opportunities are steered to the very top performers. But, again, in valuing both your clients and your people, it isn't a democracy.

At some point, you have to be very clear about this and somewhat unapologetic. A few of our best lawyers had a tremendous ability to build growth clients into multimillion-dollar clients. They got a lot of those opportunities because they were consistently great at it. They also didn't require a lot of management from me once an opportunity opened up. Great managers and leaders need to know who their best people are and to focus them on the most important areas and clients.

Another experience reinforced my thoughts on stacking resources around a few key areas rather than trying to do lots of little things. Early on in my career, I had a client with an incredibly successful surgery center. They then decided to build a second center across town. Now, rather than having one great center, the company had two fair-to-underperforming centers. It was like splitting two face cards in blackjack—turning one great hand into two weak ones. It made the client's business more difficult to manage, and it reinforced my perspective around concentration and stacking resources. It led me to think constantly about stacking resources around a handful of great conferences versus trying to hold too many. It also led me to abhor the concept of geo-cloning—expanding for expansion's sake by duplicating locations rather than deepening strength in one.

In the law practice, it led me to favor fewer, deeper offices; I wanted lots of lawyers in a few locations so they could grow a destination practice there. I came to believe that it was much easier to build a strong, aligned team when we had several lawyers concentrated in each key city—for example, twenty plus in Chicago and a similar number in Charlotte and Richmond—than if we had one or two spread across eight or ten different locations. Similarly, I wanted people stacked around a few practice areas, not dabbling with a little bit of expertise in a lot of different industries and niches.

To this day, I avoid developing too many internal teams. Instead, we constantly stack resources around the several most important areas of the company.

CHAPTER 14

The Best Founders Know Their Own Businesses

Many leaders spend a lot of time trying to follow the external environment. That can be a good thing. However, the very best leaders also know their own companies incredibly well. If they do both, they can see how their company makes its mark in the outside world. But many leaders don't spend enough time on their own company and what it does well; instead, they spend too much time distracted by external events and possible disruptions. Starting from within is the better bet.

I recall an early leader I worked with in the surgery center business: Bruce St. John. One of his team members once remarked that if a two-by-four fell in their San Antonio center, Bruce St. John would know it before they did. Bruce knew his business and operations inside and out.

This doesn't mean you want to be a micromanager. I am not a micromanager anymore—you will recall the employee who asked me if I wanted to go back to doing her job myself—and I don't encourage micromanaging. However, great founders and leaders stay very close to their business. They study and know who their most valuable leaders and employees are, who their most important customers are, and which product lines drive the most revenue and profit. They then spend a ton of time and energy on these most important areas. It's very important that they don't waste their time and energy on the areas of the business that don't move it. In fact, a key role of the leader is to know what to say no to and what not to focus attention on. Much like I hate to see a leader focusing on the 10 percent that a 90 percenter does poorly, I want our leaders concentrating their energies and resources on their most important people, customers, and business areas.

Many executive leaders can get themselves distracted with outside interests or with constantly looking for the next new thing. Many leaders want to feel important and join all kinds of different peer groups. This can be helpful in doses, but it is much less important than spending time being deeply involved in knowing your own business.

When I see a founder commission a big study or consulting project around a market area or idea, I almost always think it's a waste of time. In fact, it often leads me to lose confidence in the leader and to stop investing in the business.

Some leaders love spending time with lawyers and consultants. I often think they enjoy this because it's a distraction from the core parts of their business and the tasks that really matter. When I hear a CEO I work with saying they spoke to this law firm and this consultant, I want to scream that they should be spending that time with their employees and customers. (Most of the time I hold myself back from screaming . . . most of the time.)

When a leader spends more time on external studies and consulting or legal projects than they spend on the core business, I often think the leader is "playing at business" or acting the part of a CEO versus really trying to drive the business forward.

My high school wrestling coach used to say, "Do you actually want to wrestle, or do you just want to be on the team and pretend to be a wrestler?" (As a side note, I was a fair wrestler at best.) When I see someone acting the part of the founder versus really trying to execute on the business, I am reminded of this mantra. Is someone *playing* business leader or *being* a business leader?

I love leaders who are doer-managers or doer-leaders. They need not be completely in the trenches, but I do want them very closely aligned with those doing the job and spending serious time with top employees and top customers. No offense to ivory towers, but we don't want our leaders in them.

CHAPTER 15

Boards of Directors

This chapter, like the next chapter on taking outside money, is fairly short. That's because my core thoughts on the topic don't require much in the way of introduction—though they do require real effort in their application.

My experience with boards comes from boards within our own companies and from serving on privately held and private equity–funded boards. At Becker's Healthcare, we've had boards both prior to and after taking outside funding. Here are some pointers I've picked up along the way.

1. Keep relatively small boards of directors in which members are active. This is in contrast to the type of board that has ten to twenty board members with appointments that seem somewhat ceremonial or like rewards. I don't want big-name board members who aren't helpful.

2. Building a real business requires surrounding yourself with great advisors. Appoint board members as you start to become more of a real business in need of ongoing guidance from experienced people you deeply trust.

LinkedIn co-founder Reid Hoffman has described trust and candor as central to the chair–CEO relationship and has said his role as executive chairman was to stay closely in sync with the CEO while being willing to challenge his ideas.[37]

As we started to build a board, we were getting to the spot where we needed to better understand how to scale and how to grow our business to another level. We needed smart board members who would care about the business and had experience in growing and running others. It worked out for us; we had great outside board members and still do.

3. Strong early board members can have outsized influence. Our initial board of directors included Jessica Cole, myself, and three outside board members. One was a true entrepreneur who had built a great business. We had many of the same fears, anxieties, and thoughts. He was so helpful in so many ways. He has since passed away. The other two were great leaders who had successfully scaled great companies that ultimately sold for nearly $1 billion each. These board members were trusted mentors to Jessica and me, credible sounding boards, and incredibly helpful. All three of these board members were instrumental to us on a wide range of issues.

4. Like team members, you never know how helpful board members will be until you actually work with them. As a side note, if a potential board member wants the CEO's job or was a former CEO who may want to return, they probably shouldn't be on your board. This tends to end poorly.

5. Great board members will know your business very well, but they will also know business in general. Great board members often act as a mix of business coaches and therapists. They will be largely selfless in looking out for the business. When a board member keeps looking for what is in it for them, you might need a replacement.

6. Prior to bringing in outside capital, you are likely to have great control over who joins your board. Not so after. Once you bring in investors, you will have less control. We have been fortunate to have a great board of supportive board members from our private equity fund after taking on outside capital.

7. Your board members must be confident enough to tell you what they think versus just what you want to hear. As Scott Weiss of the venture capital firm Andreessen Horowitz emphasizes, "Quiet is not helpful. A Melvin

Milquetoast who sits there nodding his head all meeting is not helpful. I wanted someone who consistently contributed meaningfully and constructively . . . [and] who will speak up and help you build your business."[38] Sycophants and yes-men or yes-women are not going to do anyone any good.

8. A helpful board is consistently engaged. To have your board be helpful, they must be regularly involved and have a regular cadence of meetings. Staying regular and on task can be the hardest thing for a board full of busy people, but it's the difference between boards that work and boards that rubber-stamp.

9. Keep meetings tight. I'm a huge believer in shorter versus longer board meetings. I want to use board meetings to bring the board up to speed and then focus on the discussion of key issues. Great leaders and boards should be able to focus on a handful of the most critical issues versus trying to catalog all of them. I hate the four-hour board meeting. The one-hour, hyper-focused board meeting gets my vote every time.

10. Board members should be cautious about making unneeded work for the executive team. Their role is to provide strategic direction, not to micromanage or distract leaders from core priorities. As a leader, you work hard to set the agenda and keep the company focused on its most important goals. The more effectively you do this, the more autonomy the board is likely to grant you in running the business.

11. If you are on a board, you need to understand that you are a board member and not an operator. The best board members do not overstep into day-to-day execution.

12. When you are on a board, it's critical to know when it's time to step down and when you no longer add value. For most of us, there comes a time when the value that we can add dissipates. Better to be celebrated for valuable service than to be remembered as the board member who clung to their seat years after they stopped being useful.

CHAPTER 16

Outside Funding

Outside funding is a thorny issue, or it can be. There are many different perspectives on this subject, so please take my thoughts with a grain of salt. I have experienced the complexity of outside funding as a founder myself. I have also observed it firsthand at companies where I've served on the board and at others where I've advised.

I started Becker's Healthcare around 1994. At the time, I was at the predecessor law firm to McGuire-Woods. That firm was hesitant to support the marketing efforts of a young lawyer. Thus, I ended up funding the efforts for the first conferences and newsletters myself. This was well before the recent inflationary era. It was expensive then, but not by today's dollars. Over the years, my colleague and then business partner Jessica Cole became an owner in the company with me.

We were fortunate to become profitable fairly early and to self-fund the business for the first twenty-plus years. This had the benefit of allowing us to keep control of our decision-making. It also enabled my partner and me to maintain, for a long period of time, the substantial majority of ownership. This ultimately worked out well for us and left me as a huge fan of waiting to take on outside equity and funding.

In 2017, for a variety of reasons, we got serious about seeking an outside investor. We both wanted to de-risk (take some money off the table) and grow the company further. We hired an investment bank and spoke to nearly twenty potential investors. Some were strategic investors, and some were private equity funds.

We ended up completing a transaction with a private equity fund. The deal allowed us to keep a good deal of ownership of the company and retrieve some money from the table, as we had hoped. The fund and its board members have been excellent advisors. We have enjoyed a really good relationship with that fund over a fairly long period of time.

Paul Graham of Y Combinator has a great quote on the timing of raising funds in his 2005 essay "How to Fund a Startup:" "A typical startup goes through several rounds of funding, and at each round you want to take just enough money to reach the speed where you can shift into the next gear. Few startups get it quite right. Many are underfunded. A few are overfunded, which is like trying to start driving in third gear."[39]

We were able to hold off on bringing in outside equity largely because I had an outside income from my law practice and because the business was cash-flow positive. We also grew incrementally for a long period of time and didn't have huge capital needs.

WHY AND WHEN

The longer you hold on to the equity, the longer you can grow on your terms. That said, the longer you hold on to all or most of your equity, the more your net worth becomes concentrated in your business and the more risk you have that something could go wrong and cause you financial harm. Further, it's stressful to maintain two jobs while funding your business. This approach also limits your growth and your ability to add capital to take bigger risks.

When you consider taking on outside funding, you first need to assess why you are doing it. Do you want capital to put into the business to fund growth? Do you want capital so the founder and leadership team can take money off the table and de-risk? Do you need a venture capital or private equity partner that can add guidance and business help? All or some of the above?

Whatever your motivation, wait until you have real traction to raise capital. Without a clear route to revenue or scale, you risk trading long-term value for short-term cash. AngelList founder Naval Ravikant is credited with an unambiguous statement on this point: "Don't raise money until you have a clear path to revenue or scale. Otherwise, you're just selling your company's future at a discount."

In the very early stages of a business—prior to profits and sometimes prior to revenues—companies raise money from family and friends, early-stage investors, and venture capital funds. At this early point, it's more likely they need the money for growth. But for most early-stage founders, unless they have a great track record of success, raising funds tends to be much more time-consuming and difficult than expected. As venture capitalist and author Richard Harroch is said to have advised, "It's almost always harder to raise capital than you thought it would be, and it always takes longer. So plan for that."

WHO

As a company reaches profitability and starts to bring in serious earnings, the more typical investor may be private equity or a buyer in the same industry. Today, the investor landscape also includes independent sponsors, family offices, private credit firms, and banks.

Whether you're trying to bring in money to grow or to take some off the table, in most private equity transactions it's highly likely that the founders and leadership team will maintain a substantial amount of equity.

Traditionally, private equity funds will buy a majority interest and also use a finance firm to recapitalize the company with debt.

For example, let's say the company is valued at $200 million and a private equity fund is purchasing 60 percent of it. The fund will not invest $120 million directly. Instead, the company might borrow $100 million from a bank or private credit firm. This borrowing reduces the company's net equity value to $100 million. The private equity fund can then acquire its 60 percent stake for $60 million. In this scenario, the founding owners would retain 40 percent ownership and receive proceeds from both the sale and the bank financing.

When you bring in outside investors, there are three key considerations you'll want to keep in mind:

1. What is the price, what is the value, and what are the terms of the deal?

2. Can you work with and live with the partner? Are your outside investors good people, or are they sharp-elbowed and aggressive? I recently watched an outstanding founder and leader get pushed aside. The fund sought to merge the company with another business; however, the founder was reluctant to pursue that path. Whether the founder was right or not, once you give up control, you have to worry about how you and your investors will approach issues and resolve conflicts.

3. Will the investor close the deal and do what they say they will do? On that note, can the investor add value to the business? When looking at investors, I break them down into categories. Are they transformative investors or "ride-with-you" partners? Either can be great; it largely depends on what you want from an outside partner. Different private equity funds have very different approaches.

A transformative investor may want to merge you with several other companies or quickly bring in additions to the management team. They often want to do big things quickly. A ride-with-you partner will support bolt-on acquisitions—or those smaller, tuck-in deals—and organic growth. They generally don't look to totally transform the business, at least in the short term.

Some would say money is money—take the highest offer you can get from outside capital. My perspective here differs based on whether or not you are fully cashing out and exiting ownership. The closer you are to fully cashing out, the more valuation and closability become your paramount concerns.

In other words, when you bring in an outside investor, you want to make sure they offer and pay you a fair price. You also want to make sure they are likely to close the deal on the terms you have agreed to. Some buyers and investors have much better track records of closing on deals they bring to the letter-of-intent stage than others. Finally, you want to make sure the investor will be constructive and reliable to work with after they become partners with you.

The more you plan to continue working with the company, the more you should like working with the people involved. There are so many horror stories about companies that have sold to difficult funds and found it to be a horrible mistake. It's been said a million times, but I'll say it again: You can't do a good deal with bad people. Who you take funding from matters. You want to be comfortable with them. You also want to check their references and speak directly and deeply with other companies they've invested in. You don't have to love your financial partners, but they need to be decent people.

IF YOU'RE SURE...

Once you take in outside funding, even if it's a minority interest, you are less likely to have the same control you previously had. In fact, you almost certainly won't. To put it bluntly: Things will never be the same. But with the right partner, they can still be great. This makes outside funding more than a one-time decision; it's a long-term commitment. A useful warning sometimes shared by investors is that raising money is like getting married—you're committing to live with the consequences for a long time.

When you bring in outside money, you will need smart advisors who you trust to negotiate all aspects of the deal with you. You also need to really understand the tax consequences of the transaction. Always remember that, for most founders, negotiating an investment or transaction happens only a few times in the journey. In contrast, most buyers and investors spend their time negotiating deals for a living. Regardless of how gifted you are, most founders will be outmatched in negotiations unless you bring in an investment banker or advisor to negotiate for you.

For most serious deals, you will need a law firm, an investment banking firm, and a tax and accounting firm. All are expensive. There will be a temptation to save money by going cheap on advisers or to consider not using a banker at all. This is almost always a mistake. In choosing advisors, talk to a few of each type. Ask direct and difficult questions. Speak to several of their references as well. This is not a decision to take lightly.

You also want the right advisers for your specific deal. Someone who has worked in your field is excellent, but just as important is that they are used to operating within the financial range that you're in. If you are doing a $10 million or $100 million deal, you don't want a firm that usually does $1 billion deals.

CONCLUSION

Outside funding can be a catalyst or a curse. It depends on timing, motive, and partner. The best founders I know (and my own experience bears this out) wait as long as possible before taking on investors. The longer you can self-fund and grow, the stronger your negotiating position and the better your understanding of what kind of partner you truly need will be.

When you do decide to bring in outside capital, clarity matters more than speed. Know why you're raising funds, what success will look like, and who you want alongside you when the inevitable challenges arise. A fair valuation and good terms are important, but integrity, temperament, and shared vision matter even more.

Taking outside money is never just a financial transaction—it's a strategic and emotional commitment that changes how you lead and what you control. Done well, it can unlock the next chapter of growth and help you build a more durable enterprise. Done hastily, it can erode the independence and focus that made the business successful in the first place.

Be patient. Be selective. And when the right opportunity arrives, be ready.

CHAPTER 17

Twenty of My Favorite Business Concepts

This last chapter wraps up the book with a discussion of the concepts I think about most often—and that I regularly try to apply and reflect upon in my own businesses.

1. LEADERS AND FOUNDERS SHOULD LARGELY BE JUDGED ON THREE CORE THINGS.

One, there is no getting around the fact that a leader must deliver results. If a leader doesn't meet their goals and objectives, it will be hard to remain a leader for long.

Two, a leader should be judged by how many other leaders they develop. When a leader or founder develops numerous other leaders, a company can go much further. It becomes much more stable and much less fragile.

As business speaker and author John C. Maxwell argues, leadership isn't about amassing followers—it's about developing other leaders.[40]

Three, a founder or CEO should be judged by how well the organization does after the leader is gone. A leader who has built an organization that thrives when he or she retires means that he or she has built a solid company and leadership pipeline.

For this third point, look at Steve Jobs, Bill Gates, and Jeff Bezos. They each hit home runs. They built deep teams, and their organizations all excelled after they left leadership or, in the case of Steve Jobs, passed away.

2. IN EVERY STARTUP BUSINESS, THERE IS A STRESSFUL GRAY ZONE.

This is the period of time when a business has reached revenues and maybe even profitability, but it is still too dependent on a few key employees or a few key customers. This can be a very stressful time for founders. There is almost no way around the need to try and get a little bigger to try and become less fragile.

I don't have any stats on this, but I assume this early stage—when a business is very fragile, there are a million things to do, and the leader hasn't yet built a leadership team or a stable, reliable customer base—is the time when a founder is most likely to have a heart attack. I say this a bit tongue-in-cheek, but I think there is some real truth to it.

3. GREAT COMPANIES AREN'T BUILT ALONE.

I do believe that many businesses start with a highly charged firestarter of a person. You need that spark and drive to turn zero into one, as Peter Thiel writes.[41] However, that supernova founder needs to build a team.

I have seen too many companies die on the vine when they are too reliant on one person. I remember serving on the board of a supernova business. The company ultimately exited for a few million dollars. In contrast, another company I served on the board of had a CEO who incrementally built an amazing team. That company later sold for more than $800 million. The leadership structure wasn't the only difference between the two companies, but it was at the root of most of the meaningful discrepancies. I am not a believer in the one-man army, the solopreneur.

4. KNOW WHEN TO TURN OFF THE LIGHTS.

As we discussed earlier, in "The Gambler," Kenny Rogers sings, "You've got to know when to hold 'em, know when to fold 'em, know when to walk away, know when to run."[42]

Any founder who self-funds a business should look at it like a player at a blackjack table. He or she must set limits as to how much net worth they are willing to pour into the business and potentially lose. I have watched people sell income-producing assets to fund money-losing businesses. A founder needs to know when to walk away. I have seen several founders devastated financially and emotionally because they couldn't walk away from the business as it continued to drain their net worth.

In many situations, founders may feel like they can't walk away because it seems like they are just about to turn a corner. Some founders really need straight-talking advisers to help them here. Marc Andreessen and Andreessen Horowitz partners have discussed the importance of raising capital from a position of strength—before it becomes urgent.[43]

5. CASH FLOW IS KING.

For most startup founders, the goal is simple: get to the spot where monthly revenues exceed monthly expenses—where cash in exceeds cash out. Some might think this is so basic that it's not worth saying.

Not so fast.

Many founders constantly rationalize why their business is not cash-flow positive. They will say, "This type of business takes twenty-six months to get profitable," or "We really need to just add this or add that, and then we will be better positioned." An urgent goal for every founder is to get cash-flow positive . . . not to move the goalposts. If you keep raising your monthly expenses, making it harder to get to cash-flow positive, you may just be fooling yourself.

There are a few exceptions to the cash-flow positive rule. Venture capital–funded companies are often funded with the concept of putting scale before profitability. When their revenue growth starts to plateau, they (by design) try to right-size the business and get to profitability. But from the outset, their first goal is scale—not profits.

You will recall that the typical startup moves forward in five stages: idea, product, revenue, profit, and scale. With a venture capital–funded business, profits and cash flow are secondary to scale for a substantial period of time. Many founders often can't figure out how to intelligently deploy the capital that venture capital wants them to put to work; they can even be criticized for deploying it too slowly. I recall a brilliant early-stage founder who had raised capital from a top-notch venture capital firm. He was astounded by the pressure the VC fund put on him to put that money to work.

To take one step back to the funnel concept—idea to product to revenues to profits to scale—many founders can't manage to turn their idea into a product or a real business. Nolan Bushnell, founder of Atari, has been credited with a quote on this concept that resonates with me:

"The critical ingredient is getting off your butt and doing something. It's as simple as that. A lot of people have ideas, but there are few who decide to do something about them now. Not tomorrow. Not next week. But today."[44]

6. SET TARGETS AND GOALS THAT WORK.

There are very different views on how companies should set revenue, profit, and other goals. One school of thought says the founder should set big, hairy, audacious goals (thanks, Jim Collins!). Sometimes there is a machismo to this that almost belittles the CEO or founder who doesn't want to set stretch goals like that.

A second view of goal setting ascribes more value to the concept that a company should set rational, challenging, but realistic goals and try to keep on beating them.

By nature, I am an incrementalist. I largely think in terms of the second method—setting rational and achievable goals. In my experience, this helps leaders and organizations build confidence. It's very similar, mentally, to how cash flow works. If you get to cash-flow positive, you can take on all kinds of growth initiatives and opportunities. You can also be cautious in taking on outside capital; then you don't have external pressure to do anything. Similarly, if you set goals and keep hitting them, you can keep setting more goals toward bigger targets. You gain confidence and get better and better.

Kevin O'Leary, a prolific and successful investor across numerous ventures, has strong thoughts on goal setting. He also has opinions on why he often has biases toward women CEOs over males. In short, he has had more success with women CEOs—he believes they more often set realistic goals and achieve them, which builds confidence. Male CEOs, on the other hand, often set stretch goals they don't meet. Even though the company may still perform well, consistently falling short of these stretch goals is deflating to the team. He said this regarding setting goals and building companies: "When you're on a team and you hit your targets every quarter, it gets very sticky. People want to stay on the team, just like if you were playing for Brady during the six Super Bowl rings. You don't wanna get traded. You're hitting your bonuses, and you're getting paid. You feel good about yourself. So, these businesses had no disruption in business, and that's why they had superior returns."[45]

In business, founders and CEOs will also face pressure from investors, bankers, and others as to how to set projections. An investment banker may want a CEO or founder who is going to set aggressive projections to try and push for a higher valuation. An investor may want the same thing, either when going to market or when trying to raise more bank financing.

Either way, a CEO or founder has to push back on this when he or she feels the goals are not rational. This is psychologically important. It also can have legal implications. This is often a more delicate situation than people would like to acknowledge.

7. GRATITUDE IS A CORE TRAIT AND ATTITUDE.

Founders maintain a fascinating balance; they need people to get things done, and at the same time they need people they want to work with and who in turn enjoy working for the company. Compensation may be one core lever toward getting the right people to work for a company and remaining aligned therewith. However, as anyone who has run a company knows, it takes a lot more than compensation to keep people aligned and working in unison.

Over a long period, I have come to a few core concepts about the temperament and attitude of a founder.

First, a core manner of dealing with customers and team members is through immense, sincere, and deep gratitude. In the old days, you showed gratitude through a paycheck. Make no mistake: The right level of compensation remains important. But compensation is just one part of the table stakes for bringing people in and retaining them. Money is just a puzzle piece. The leaders must remain constantly grateful to their best employees and to all their employees in general. The same gratitude must be shown to their vendors and partners.

A phrase often attributed to Peter Drucker "Culture eats strategy for breakfast" is better as a plaque than an actual operating paradigm. Generally, I believe it's more aptly stated, "Culture *plus* talent *plus* strategy eats any one of them for breakfast." But as to culture, I want leaders who constantly see the good and not the bad in their team members. As stated earlier, I look for those who can truly appreciate their 90 percenters and focus overwhelmingly on that priceless 90 percent.

Likewise, that gratitude shouldn't be a secret. I want a leader who is focused on constantly letting people know how much they are appreciated. Over the years, I have received so many lessons in this that resonated with me and led me to constantly praise our terrific performers. I got so zealous in my gratitude that one great leader tried to nickname me "The Thank-You Man."

Don't get me wrong, people who know me well might say I have a good heart, but none would call me Zen or super sweet. Rather, I find myself genuinely grateful to clients and customers and the teams who make it all work. When you truly and deeply have this perspective of gratitude, it makes it easier to show it every day.

8. EVERY ORGANIZATION NEEDS A POLICE PERSON OR AN ACCOUNTABILITY LEADER.

Some may take issue with this idea. To be clear, when I talk about a group needing a police officer, I don't mean that businesses are Gucci stores in need of police outside to stop burglars. Rather, I use the term to mean that every company needs people within it to hold teams and people accountable.

We need people and supervisors who are focused on making sure our teams get the right amount of work completed. In the conference business, we need people making sure we get the right number of registrants to every event or activity. They need to sit down with people and set the proper goals. Then they need to check in regularly to make sure those goals are met.

When building a company, you may get negative feedback about this or the people who are serving in this role. In my experience—and this is absolutely my experience—the supervisor who is holding people accountable is doing what has to be done. Of course you have some supervisors who are too harsh. However, more often than not I'd say I have had too many supervisors who were too soft. This by no means implies that a police person can break rules or cross the line themselves. But someone in organizations needs to hold people responsible.

I vividly remember receiving some lobbying for the firing of a person who held people accountable. Two younger writers complained about how demanding the leader was. This is where founders need to make some judgment calls: Are the demands reasonable? If so, how is the manager behaving in enforcing them? In this case, my perception was that the leader was right on. In fact, the person was so much right on that they have grown into a ride-or-die leader over the last twelve years.

It's my experience that the person who holds people accountable will periodically come under criticism. When someone gets on the warpath regarding an enforcer, I explain the importance of what that leader does and ask the person criticizing them if they want that job.

If the CEO has to be the chief accountability officer as well, it is likely to exhaust them. A CEO needs to be highly engaged in working with the company's leaders; he or she needs to help set strategy and make decisions; and he or she has to work with the board and investors and face the public. For an organization to thrive, a CEO has to excel. Thus, to be a great CEO and make sure the organization thrives, the CEO needs a separate COO as well as department leaders who police accountability.

9. EMBRACE ADDITION BY SUBTRACTION.

In every organization I have ever been part of, there are either customers or team members who are so time-consuming for leadership or who treat others so poorly that the organization would simply be better off without them.

There is always a perception that the loss of such a person will leave a void or that the loss of the customer will mean a hit to revenues. However, it has been my experience that letting those employees go or terminating those client relationships is very positive for the company, both immediately and in the long term.

We have spoken a lot about having enough depth in terms of both team members and clients. Another core reason you need depth in both areas is so that you don't have to tolerate team members or clients who are difficult to work with.

A banner day in the development of any business is the day you don't have to take on every customer who will do business with you. You can fire clients who don't pay their bills or are very difficult on your people. I remember these moments vividly.

Similarly, you can build a deep enough team that you can hold people accountable or terminate those who become a cancer to the organization. A brilliant surgeon leader named Dan Murray said to me nearly two decades ago that he needed at least twenty orthopedic surgeons in a group so that he couldn't be held hostage by the few surgeons who were incredibly difficult or who would hold the group back. Similarly, I recall getting to the spot in the law practice where we had enough business that I could tell a client that they couldn't treat our people rudely.

10. "NOBODY RIDES FOR FREE."

Again, this phrase appeals to me on several levels. In the media business, companies constantly ask you to highlight them, even if they are not advertisers or sponsors. Each one pitches us the same thing: They are so special as to be newsworthy—we should amplify what they do in a non-paid way.

At some point, we made it very clear that the companies we work with help us pay the bills and keep the lights on—"nobody rides for free." The same is true of team members. Everyone must contribute something.

11. SMART PRICING MATTERS.

As a somewhat sales-driven entrepreneur by nature, I have always gravitated toward lower prices to bring customers in and grow the business. As I have worked with great CEOs and boards over the years, I have learned that these instincts do not always provide the right answer in the long term. Rather, you need to be in businesses that charge enough that you can hire and keep great people. Very simply, you need two things in most businesses: great customers and great team members. If you don't price well enough, you can't build the right team and do things in an exceptional way.

As a founder and entrepreneur, it was hard for me to learn to raise prices to the point that allowed us to do business the way we wanted to do it. I am generally a believer in raising prices incrementally, but like the concept of "nobody rides for free," you need strong enough and fair enough pricing to hire and keep and build the team you want. Sometimes you have to make a jump.

If you have plenty of work but thin profits, the remedy is simple: raise your prices. Said a different way—and this goes back to the concept of addition by subtraction—most businesses benefit by getting rid of their lowest-paying customers and focusing more and more resources on their best customers. I remember a brilliant colleague in the landscaping business getting rid of their twenty most challenging customers so they could better serve their best clients. I loved this.

12. IT'S HARD TO BUILD A BUSINESS, AND IT'S VERY HARD TO STAY ON TOP.

One of the best, simplest lessons from the famous founder of Intel, Andy Grove, is that it is very hard to build a business, and it is just as hard to remain a top and leading business. Andy titled one of his books *Only the Paranoid Survive*.[46] To me, this means that if you want to remain a great business, it will take almost maniacal work over a long period of time to stay successful.

Intel was the top name in computer chips for a long time. Now firms like Nvidia are far more advanced. In contrast, companies like Epic, Microsoft, and Apple have been obsessive about staying at the top of their game. Amazon is a great example of a firm motivated to dually test new areas and get better in its core business.

Jim Collins, the brilliant author of *Good to Great*, has another impactful book on how great companies fail as well: *How the Mighty Fall: And Why Some Companies Never Give In.*[47]

I have been in one business for more than thirty years, and I can't express enough how great a team you must build and how hungry and excited that team must remain to stay great over a long period of time. The company must keep recruiting and keep trying to get better. Yes, you need to refresh and relax from time to time—but the company can't afford to do so for very long and expect to stay great.

13. IT'S HARD TO GET RICH AND VERY HARD TO STAY RICH.

This concept falls a bit outside the gamut of startup discussions, but it remains one I find interesting. It is somewhat tied to how successful people can fail financially.

Many startup founders get their first touch of wealth through their startup. Some start to believe they have the Midas touch. They think they will be successful in their next ventures as well. They can spend freely, because they will simply do it again next time.

They don't realize how much easier it is to go broke than it is to get rich.

Jim Collins discusses this extensively. He says the newly rich chase more fame and status and that wealth breeds overconfidence. In any event, one of the best pieces of advice I got after my first real exit was to avoid any substantial spending for at least a year. Likewise, I taught myself to love a conservative portfolio, even when I missed the upside of some great markets. Easy come, easy go. Difficult come, easy go.

14. KEEP TWO BALANCE SHEETS.

Closely related to the last point, I am also a huge believer that a founder should work to be financially secure both inside and outside the business. If a founder builds a real business, they will essentially have two balance sheets: their personal finances and their share of the company.

My sense is that the founder who builds both is far better positioned to do two key things. First, he or she can keep taking risks, growing the business, hiring people, and taking new initiatives because he or she is financially safe outside the business. Second, a founder who continues to mind their net worth outside the business can remain safe if the business does go sideways.

15. GREAT PARTNERS TAKE YOU FURTHER.

Over time I came to the very clear conclusion that businesses can go much further and be much more satisfying with a great partner or partners. As a self-starter and founder, I embraced this gradually over time—then fully. I ended up with fantastic partners at Becker's Healthcare and McGuireWoods. Quite frankly, I have been lucky to hit it out of the park with great long-term partners. Finding and cultivating great long-term partners is no sure thing, similar to finding and cultivating great team members.

You don't meet someone and become partners. You work closely with someone, and over time it emerges that this person is a great fit as a partner both business-wise and personality-wise. You can respect each other, not drive each other crazy, and stay determined and aligned on what you are trying to accomplish. Over the long run, nothing (or next to nothing) is as important as a great partner.

16. "NO NEW IDEAS" CAN BE A GREAT IDEA.

One of my favorite concepts in business is designating periods of "no new ideas." This concept can be much maligned, but I believe there are simply times that need to be blocked out for "no new ideas."

When a company is heavily focused on a core priority, I want my people focused on execution—not distracted by new ideas and new initiatives. When trying to get something big done, we don't want everyone brainstorming and making new suggestions. Further, when someone starts with the company, I largely want them learning what is going on and getting their feet wet before they start giving their supervisors new ideas. I know this can sound like a Neanderthal way of doing business, but it stands alongside the concept that when a company has clear priorities, it isn't chasing a million different things.

I've watched founders look at starting multiple service lines when they should be focused on making their core service line great and keeping their expenses in line. Some may think this seems basic and overstated, but I have so often seen the distraction that comes with an idea-a-minute way of life that I consciously avoid and prohibit new ideas during key periods of execution.

There is an old adage that says there are no dumb ideas and no dumb questions. I wholeheartedly disagree!

17. SIMPLICITY IS IMPERATIVE.

Two of my favorite quotes related to simplicity are as follows. First, former professional golfer Nancy Lopez says, "The simpler I keep things, the better I play."[48] Second, Becker's Healthcare CEO Jessica Cole says, "We teach the highlighter method." To take this concept one step further, Mark Twain famously quoted Shakespeare's *Hamlet* in saying, "Brevity is the soul of wit."

As a leader, I operate at my very best when I can simplify things. In law, we used to say it was a very simple business: We just needed great lawyers and great clients. That entire business was built around finding and recruiting both. In media, we need a great audience plus great customers who want to meet that audience. We often say we need to be a magnet for attendees, readers, and listeners.

In everything you do, the more you can keep it simple—or as Gary Keller says, focus on the one thing that matters—the better you are. Greg McKeown has a great book on this topic called *Essentialism*.[49] Every time I have had a great success, I have been able to focus on very few things and obsessively dive into that simplicity. In contrast, every time I have performed in an average way, I have been trying to do too much and have not made things simple. I overthink things often. The more we in business can bounce back to simplicity, the better off we are by far.

18. FAILURE IS FINE WITHIN REASON.

In any business, we want leaders who constantly take shots at the fence, start new initiatives, and hire new leaders. We want them to be confident that even if one thing doesn't work out, they should still take chances on the next.

I view hiring as an educated gamble. The last thing I want is a leader making a hire that doesn't work out and then becoming gun-shy about hiring in general. Companies like Amazon have grown on the concept of trying new initiatives and then making the decision to double down, shut it down, or stay the course. When I see them fail to excel in retail or healthcare, I don't really view that as failure. Rather, I see it as part of their core business—they test different areas and then proceed according to the results.

The counter to this is another brilliant thought from Jim Collins. He says to fire bullets, not cannons. The idea is that if you test a hire or an initiative and it doesn't work, you haven't done large damage to the company. Measured risk and failure are within reason. That said, a leader who keeps failing or who fails big probably has a limited runway as a leader.

19. THE POWER OF "NO-BLAME CULTURES."

I believe in "no-blame cultures." This goes hand in hand with the idea of loving your 90 percenters. Unless someone really messes something up or regularly makes an error that they clearly understood better than to make, I largely want to refrain from talking to them about it. And I definitely don't want to call them out publicly.

Every interaction can be positive or negative. If I regularly tell someone they made this typo or this error, my guess is the recipient will grow to hate me, my practices, or the whole business. I experience this with readers, for example, who feel the need to message me each morning and say, "Hey, I thought you would want to know about this mistake." It's complicated, because they may mean well, and it may even be helpful sometimes . . . but I kind of can't stand it when they do this.

As a leader, my key goal is overwhelmingly focusing on what people are doing right and largely ignoring a weakness or error unless there is some real benefit to discussing it. If something is going to hold back their career, we need to discuss it; if something is a mere inconvenience for me, but that person is a driving engine for the business, the less said the better.

20. THERE IS ONE TRICK TO GREAT MANAGEMENT.

I have found that there is a very simple trick to great management. Hire great people. If you are a coach and have a great team, your job is to make the most of that talent. If you don't have great people, you likely need to manage very closely—and even then, there is a clear ceiling as to how much you can do.

I have watched some great leaders shun the effort to work with bright, motivated people. They have still been able to turn out great work; it may even have been the best way for them to manage. But from my perspective, it's a ton easier to work with really gifted people who you do not have to manage so closely. Both tight and loose management can work, but I have found that the best way to be a great coach—like Phil Jackson, coach of the six-time champion Chicago Bulls—is to have players like Michael Jordan on your team. That's a metaphor, as that type of talent isn't something you are likely to have every day. But it's a lot easier to be a great manager when you have great people.

CONCLUSION

We've loved our business journey—it's been full of ups and downs, challenges, and countless lessons learned. Our hope is that you have enjoyed this book and that some of the concepts and ideas within it prove useful as you build your business, team, and career. We're huge fans of entrepreneurs and leaders, and we're deeply grateful to you for reading. Thank you.

APPENDIX
Fifteen Business Books
Worth Reading

This is not intended to be a definitive list of the greatest business books of all time. Rather, it's a personal list—business books I've read and returned to time and again over the years. Each one has offered something practical, insightful, or grounding during different stages of building and leading businesses.

The Go-Giver: A Little Story About a Powerful Business Idea
Bob Burg and John David Mann
(Portfolio, 2007)

Good to Great: Why Some Companies Make the Leap . . . And Others Don't
Jim Collins
(Harper Business, 2001)

The 7 Habits of Highly Effective People: Powerful Lessons in Personal Change
Stephen R. Covey
(Free Press, 1989)

The Effective Executive: The Definitive Guide to Getting the Right Things Done
Peter Drucker
(Harper & Row, 1967)

How to Become a Rainmaker: The Rules for Getting and Keeping Customers and Clients
Jeffrey J. Fox
(Hyperion, 2000)

The Hard Thing About Hard Things: Building a Business When There Are No Easy Answers—Straight Talk on the Challenges of Entrepreneurship
Ben Horowitz
(Harper Business, 2014)

The ONE Thing: The Surprisingly Simple Truth About Extraordinary Results
Gary Keller with Jay Papasan
(Bard Press, 2013)

The 80/20 Principle: The Secret to Achieving More with Less
Richard Koch
(Doubleday, 1998)

Essentialism: The Disciplined Pursuit of Less
Greg McKeown
(Crown Business, 2014)

Organize Tomorrow Today: 8 Ways to Retrain Your Mind to Optimize Performance at Work and in Life
Jason Selk and Tom Bartow
(Da Capo Lifelong Books, 2015)

The Art of Profitability
Adrian Slywotzky
(Warner Books, 2002)

Zero to One: Notes on Startups, or How to Build the Future
Peter Thiel with Blake Masters
(Crown Business, 2014)

Winning
Jack Welch and Suzy Welch
(Harper Business, 2005)

10–10–10: A Fast and Powerful Way to Get Unstuck in Love, at Work, and with Your Family
By Suzy Welch
(Scribner, 2009)

Profit from the Core: A Return to Growth in Turbulent Times
Chris Zook with James Allen
(Harvard Business School Press, 2010)

NOTES

1. Peter F. Drucker, *The Effective Executive: The Definitive Guide to Getting the Right Things Done* (HarperBusiness, 1997).
2. Jim Collins, *Good to Great: Why Some Companies Make the Leap . . . and Others Don't* (Harper Business, 2001).
3. Suzy Welch, *10–10–10: A Life-Transforming Idea* (Scribner, 2009).
4. Jason Fried and David Heinemeier Hansson, *Rework* (Crown Business, 2010).
5. Alex Osterwalder, "Why Lengthy Business Plans Increase the Risk of Failure," Strategyzer (blog), February 7, 2017.
6. Satya Nadella with Greg Shaw and Jill Tracie Nichols, *Hit Refresh: The Quest to Rediscover Microsoft's Soul and Imagine a Better Future for Everyone* (Harper Business, 2017).
7. Grant Cardone, *The 10X Rule: The Only Difference Between Success and Failure* (Wiley, 2011).
8. Kenny Rogers, "The Gambler," written by Don Schlitz, United Artists Records, 1978.
9. Jack Welch, comments to GE corporate officer, Crotonville, NY, February 2, 1987.

10. Adrian Slywotzky, *The Art of Profitability* (Warner Books, 2002).

11. Paul Graham, "How to Get Startup Ideas," *Paul Graham.com*, November 2012, https://paulgraham.com /startupideas.html.

12. Hernán Cortés's destruction of his ships is described in early accounts of the Spanish conquest of Mexico, including Bernal Díaz del Castillo, *The Conquest of New Spain*, trans. J. M. Cohen (London: Penguin Classics, 1963). Modern business and leadership literature commonly paraphrases this episode as "burn the boats"; attribution varies.

13. Gary Keller and Jay Papasan, *The ONE Thing: The Surprisingly Simple Truth Behind Extraordinary Results* (Bard Press, 2013).

14. Jeff Bezos, quoted in Bill Murphy Jr., "Jeff Bezos: 'We're Not Competitor Obsessed, We're Customer Obsessed,'" *Inc.*, February 4, 2023, https://www.inc.com /bill-murphy-jr/bezos-most-important-single-thing-focus -obsessively-on-customer.html.

15. Michael Dell, "Ideas are a commodity. Execution of them is not," X (formerly Twitter), September 13, 2024, https://x.com/MichaelDell/status/18345429095273 72093.

16. Peter Thiel and Blake Masters, *Zero to One: Notes on Startups, or How to Build the Future* (Crown Business, 2014).

17. Barbara Corcoran, "Don't be afraid to go for positions, jobs, or take on clients just outside of your knowledge base . . . ," Facebook, March 24, 2014, https://www .facebook.com/TheBarbaraCorcoran/posts/101522 95407249770.

18. Paul Graham, "How to Present to Investors," Paul Graham.com, August 2006 (revised April 2007, September 2010), https://www.paulgraham.com/investors.html.

19. Ben Thompson, "Teams OS and the Slack Social Network," *Stratechery*, July 7, 2020, https://stratechery.com/2020/the-slack-social-network/.

20. Eric Ries, *The Lean Startup: How Today's Entrepreneurs Use Continuous Innovation to Create Radically Successful Businesses* (New York: Crown Business, 2011).

21. Marty Cagan, "Charter Customer Programs," SVPG (Silicon Valley Product Group), August 17, 2007, https://www.svpg.com/charter-customer-programs/.

22. Kevin Ward, *Sell Like a Pro: Build a World-Class Sales Organization by Helping People Succeed* (Austin, TX: YES Masters, 2018).

23. Seth Godin, *The Bootstrapper's Bible: How to Start and Build a Business With a Great Idea and (Almost) No Money* (Upstart, 1998).

24. Peter F. Drucker, *The Effective Executive: The Definitive Guide to Getting the Right Things Done* (Harper & Row, 1966).

25. Ibid.

26. Richard Koch, *The 80/20 Principle: The Secret to Achieving More with Less* (Doubleday, 1998).

27. Michael Mankins, "Stop Focusing on Profitability and Go for Growth," *Harvard Business Review*, May 1, 2017, https://hbr.org/2017/05/stop-focusing-on-profitability-and-go-for-growth.

28. Reid Hoffman, quoted in Alyson Shontell, "LinkedIn's Reid Hoffman: If You're Not Embarrassed by Your First Product, You Launched Too Late," *Business*

Insider, May 26, 2011, https://www.businessinsider.com/reid-hoffman-if-youre-not-embarrassed-by-your-first-product-you-launched-too-late-2011-5.

29. Chris Zook and James Allen, *Profit from the Core: A Return to Growth in Turbulent Times* (Harvard Business Review Press, 2010).

30. Jack Welch and John A. Byrne, *Jack: Straight from the Gut* (Warner Business Books, 2001).

31. Paul Jarvis, *Company of One: Why Staying Small Is the Next Big Thing for Business* (Boston: Houghton Mifflin Harcourt, 2019).

32. Jack Welch and John A. Byrne, *Jack: Straight from the Gut* (New York: Warner Business Books, 2001), describing GE's "vitality curve" performance system.

33. Elise Contarsy, comment on Scott Becker, "Give me one quote or idea please . . . ," *LinkedIn*, accessed October 6, 2025.

34. Jeffrey J. Fox, *How to Become a Rainmaker: The Rules for Getting and Keeping Customers and Clients* (Hyperion, 2000).

35. Jeffrey J. Fox, *How to Become a Great Boss: The Rules for Getting and Keeping the Best Employees* (Hyperion, 2002).

36. Ibid.

37. Reid Hoffman, "If, Why, and How Founders Should Hire a 'Professional' CEO," *LinkedIn*, January 23, 2013, https://www.linkedin.com/pulse/20130123161202-1213-if-why-and-how-founders-should-hire-a-professional-ceo.

38. Scott Weiss, "The Best Board Member," Andreessen Horowitz (a16z), October 7, 2013, https://a16z.com/the-best-board-member.

39. Paul Graham, "How to Fund a Startup," PaulGraham .com, November 2005, https://paulgraham.com/startup funding.html.

40. John C. Maxwell, *Developing the Leader Within You* (Thomas Nelson, 1993).

41. Peter Thiel and Blake Masters, *Zero to One: Notes on Startups, or How to Build the Future* (Crown Business, 2014).

42. Kenny Rogers, "The Gambler," written by Don Schlitz, United Artists Records, 1978.

43. Steve McDermid, "16 Common Questions About Fundraising," Andreessen Horowitz, February 27, 2015, https:// a16z.com/16-common-questions-about-fundraising/

44. Richard Harroch, "50 Inspirational Quotes for Startups and Entrepreneurs," *Forbes*, February 10, 2014, accessed October 7, 2025, https://www.forbes.com/sites/allbusiness /2014/02/10/50-inspirational-quotes-for-startups-and -entrepreneurs.

45. Kevin O'Leary (@kevinolearytv), X (formerly Twitter), May 12, 2025, accessed October 7, 2025, https://x.com /kevinolearytv/status/1921943411793224143.

46. Andrew S. Grove, *Only the Paranoid Survive: How to Exploit the Crisis Points That Challenge Every Company* (Currency/Doubleday, 1996).

47. Jim Collins, *How the Mighty Fall: And Why Some Companies Never Give In* (HarperBusiness, 2009).

48. Nancy Lopez, *The Complete Golfer* (Galahad Books, 1989).

49. Greg McKeown, *Essentialism: The Disciplined Pursuit of Less* (Crown Business, 2014).